SON OF A
CARPENTER

Hardcover ISBN: 979-8-8229-4970-6
Paperback ISBN: 979-8-8229-4971-3

SON OF A
CARPENTER

GARY LEE

A Dedication

I'm sure you know by now that this is my first attempt at writing a book. Thank you for your patience as I muddled through. Every time I think I'm finished, a little voice in my head would say, "Not yet." Patience may be a virtue, but it's not one I possess! Obviously, the little voice knows more about this venture than I do! I want to try and close with a dedication. Please bear with me one more time.

I want to dedicate this book to my younger brother, Don. Maybe his struggles have just been magnified to me through all of this, or maybe he's the reason I have been led to write it. Even from a very young age, his "differences" stood out. He desperately sought to fit in, and that desperation just amplified his skewed behavior.

If any of his antics caused my parents to smile or laugh, he would repeat them over and over until he was told to stop, or when he was just ignored. Which happened a lot. Ignored. I keep asking myself what that must be like. To be disregarded or at least treated that way. If I try to imagine how he must have felt, all I feel is lonely. Hollow. Invisible.

I worked in a profession dedicated to helping people but couldn't make the effort to help Don. Complete strangers were given my full attention if they needed anything. He never did anything to harm me or even anger me. What caused me to treat him the way I did? How different would his life had been if I had just tried to understand him? Now I will never know.

I believe there are lots of "Don's" in the world. You probably know at least one. I can't change the way I treated him. I can't even apologize now. Maybe someone reading this will see themselves acting the way I did. Maybe it will cause people to notice the ones that live on the fringe, the square pegs in a round hole world. He didn't act out to stand out. Just the opposite. He just wanted to be noticed. To be accepted. To fit in. I could have helped. I just didn't.

Foreword

By 7:00 am the coffee maker is on its 3rd pot and an eager new firefighter or two are topping off a collection of mismatched cups strewn around an insanely long table. While shift change isn't until 8:00, the good ones are already there. The veterans are seated at the table revolving through a host of topics ranging from horrible marital advice, disdain for upper management, hazing and perhaps a little fishing or hunting. But there's also some straight business about the rigs, their district and how the night's fire went. Because some of this information is pure gold and the new guys wades through the rest with grace. You can bet my friend Gary was there and as for words, he chose quality over quantity.

My wife (an elementary teacher) jokingly says all firefighters have attention deficit disorder (ADD) and we are drawn to the chaos of FF to hide our flaws. I can't argue because she can spot us a mile away, giant mustache or not. As for me, I believe nearly all of us saw or lived something that led to a void that working the best job ever, the American fire service, so perfectly fills. Reverence for the craft is everything, quiet service is the modus operandi, no bragging, all in, and a desire for the respect of one's peers way before bugles (rank) or shine at city hall.

The fact of firefighting is that it's about 90% of the preparation but only 10% of the actual calls. The bulk of the responses are far less dramatic but still include someone having the worst day of their month, year or even life. Some of these people are having a recurring worst day. I've seen some of the most touching, poignant interventions from some of the hardest macho firefighters in these situations. Their own experiences lead to a perfect read of the situation.

Gary and I are retired now, and I was excited when he invited me to lunch. He was writing a book and asked me to read it. When I got home, I didn't stop until I was out of pages. It's a wonderful story of a far from ideal start in life and how we can be lifted to become the lifter. Enjoy the book!

Landon Stallings
Fort Worth Fire Department (Retired)

Introduction

I don't believe in coincidence. I'm not trying to change your personally held beliefs, just explaining mine. It's been my own experience that things that "just happen" always end up being extremely important in the big picture of things. I do believe that God puts people in our life when: (a) we need them; (b) they need us; or (c) we need each other. Extremely random meetings and ensuing friendships have played an amazing part in bringing all this story to life.

Last, I believe that little seeds planted years ago have been waiting to bloom. Just recently, one of those seeds has been foremost on my mind.

Walter was a deacon in the little church I grew up in. He was older than the other deacons and always wore a western cut suit and a tie. Walter had a very distinctive voice. Very bass, and a slightly gravelly tone. As a deacon, Walter was called on many times to pray. The closing portion of all his prayers were the first seeds planted in my mind.

At the close of his prayer, Walter would repeat this phrase: "Lead, Guide, and Direct us Father, in all that we do. And we give Thee all the Praise. For it's in Jesus' name we pray, Amen."

Lead. Guide. Direct. Nothing forceful, nothing demanding. Each of those words are things that I think of when I think of a loving father. It's been my experience that whenever I follow that lead, everything works for the best. Not perfect or instant. It has taken me a LOT of years to see how the plan was put in place, probably before I was even born, to put me in the right place, at just the right time, to find my purpose. I have definitely experienced God's guidance and I believe it's been His direction that put the people in my life, exactly when I needed them, that has made all the difference. I wish I could say that I always followed His lead, always let Him guide and direct me, but that would be completely false. I believe God knew I would stumble, veer way off course, and in some cases, completely turn my back on His love for me. He has never given up on me. Always loving me unconditionally. So, here is my story. I hope you like it!

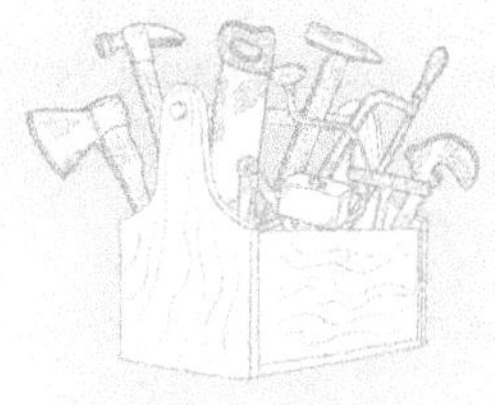

The Incident

For all practical purposes, my story began on December 22, 1974. I was 16 years old and out of school for Christmas vacation. When I say 16 years old, I mean that I had seen that many birthdays. Physically and mentally, probably closer to 13. I was extremely shy, almost to the same measure naïve, and physically a whopping 5 feet 5 inches and just over 100 lbs. I had been anxiously awaiting this day for some time now. I had spent the previous night at my friend, Jeff's, house because his stepdad Joe had promised to take us hunting. We left before sunup and drove to Palo Pinto County. Jeff's family had a lake house there, and a neighbor had agreed to let us hunt on his property. Our "hunt" consisted of walking through several fields, carrying .22 rifles and laughing and talking loud enough to warn any animals of our approach. That was okay. Neither of us fired a shot, but I doubt that any two people had as much fun as we did.

After a couple of hours, Joe brought us back to their home in Fort Worth. We were in the dining room, cutting up and Joe was fixing our lunch. Something we said got Joe tickled and he was still laughing when he answered a ringing phone. I noticed the smile left immediately left his face and the tone of his voice became very serious.

"We have to go to the hospital. Your dad has had a heart attack". I don't remember getting in the truck or the drive to the hospital. I know they talked to me on the way, but I just saw their lips moving. When you hear someone say, "it's like I was in a fog", this must be what they mean. My next recollection, where I could hear and understand, was when we got to the waiting room at John Peter Smith Hospital.

When we walked in, I saw my mom, my younger brother, and my little sister, and my mom's friend Mary. More about Mary in a minute. My mom never was affectionate, so I wasn't surprised when she didn't hug me as I approached her. She started telling me about how wonderful the firefighters were about taking care of my dad. My oldest sister and her husband came in and my mom began retelling the story of the firefighters. Every new visitor heard the same version. Maybe it took my mom's mind off the severity of the situation, almost like a defense mechanism.

Mary pulled me aside and gave me a big hug. My eyes were burning from holding back tears, but I had been brought up not to cry. Ever. I quickly rubbed my eyes to remove any trace. So far, no tears.

Mary explained that she was on the phone with my mom when my dad collapsed. My mom screamed into the phone and asked Mary what to do. Mary told her to hang up and call for an ambulance. Mary told my mom, "I will get you some help". Mary's husband had been a firefighter before leaving to start a fence building company. Mary called the fire department and asked them to please help my mom. Now remember, this was 1974. I really don't know if medical calls were part of their normal response, but they sent a firetruck. By all accounts, they did an incredible job.

Friends and neighbors stopped by over the next several hours. As the room began to clear out, someone took my mom, brother, and little sister home. My mom left me the keys to my car and told me where she had parked. Jeff had asked to stay, so, soon it was just the two of us. Jeff and I have been friends since we were around 5 years old. We grew up in the same little church. If you ever have a friend that will sleep on the floor in the waiting room of a hospital with you, hang on to them forever! I don't think I ever told Jeff how much that meant to me. I'll fix that.

Early the next morning, I took Jeff to his house and went home to clean up and change clothes. We lived on a corner lot and our side door opened toward the garage and our driveway. When I stepped out that door, a car pulled up. A man in a uniform stepped out and my heart beat faster. I had never seen a firefighter, so I assumed that this man had been sent by the hospital to deliver bad news about my dad.

As he approached our house, he identified himself as Captain Hunter. He explained that he was with the firefighters that had responded to help my dad. As he was asking about my dad's condition and asking if my mom was home, the side door flew open and my mom ran (something I had never seen), threw her arms around his neck and cried all over his uniform shirt. Capt. Hunter let her cry. The look on his face told me this was not the first time he had been in this situation. As my mom began to compose herself, he told her that his crew felt bad about this happening to us right before Christmas. He said they had all chipped in to get us a "few" things. He asked me to please help him with the box in his car. When he opened the back door, I noticed the box stretched from one side of the car to the other. It was overflowing. It looked as if they had gone up and down each aisle in the store and picked up every conceivable thing a family could use. I had heard the term "care package", but until that moment, I had never seen one.

As we carried it in the side door, I saw our little aluminum Christmas tree with the colored light wheel behind it. There were 3 small gifts under the tree. Total value less than $30. I know that because I had bought them. One was for my dad, and one each for my younger siblings. All at once, I had the revelation that I had denied for years; We were poor! Not just lower income, not having a tough time,…Poor! That same burning sensation hit my eyes again, but I wouldn't give in. Still no tears.

Capt. Hunter walked me outside and put his arm around my shoulder. He told me that I need to step up and be the man of the house for my mom and my siblings. Then he said, "Even the man of the house needs help sometimes". He gave me a card with the station phone number and his name on it. He told me to call him or the station if we needed anything. He then turned to my mom, took out his wallet and gave my mom a $100 bill. In 1974, that was a lot of money, or at least it was to us. He told my mom to use it for whatever we needed to make our Christmas better. What he didn't know was that $100 was a lifeline! It kept our utilities on, gas in the car, and money for parking at the hospital. At that moment, with as much clarity and determination as my 16-year-old self could muster, I decided that I was going to be a firefighter. Nothing was going to change my mind or keep me from it. I felt like I had a debt to repay. I was going to be the "Capt. Hunter" for someone that needed that in their life.

Every weight I lifted, and every mile I ran was meant to bring me closer to that goal. There were plenty of obstacles, several fortunate meetings, and always, yes always, God's guiding hand.

On December 22nd, 1978, exactly 4 years later, I graduated from the Fort Worth Fire Department Training Academy. Let me tell you about the days and years between and you will see what I mean when I say I don't believe in coincidences, and about how people show up in your life for a reason.

One more note about my mom's friend Mary; If my mom had been on the phone with ANYONE else, what are the odds that the firefighters would even have been called? Hmmm

My Dad's Last Days

My dad was in ICU for his entire stay. He never regained consciousness and the doctor said he probably never would. I had been making the trek to see him every day and now that school had started back, all the evening visits interfered with my job at Red Lobster. So, I quit. I never thought about having faith that I would find another job. I just thought about how I wasn't going to make the choice of work over family. Looking back, it was risky.

We had no money coming in, and the money from Capt. Hunter was almost gone. Still, I was at peace with my decision.

I belonged to a small youth group at church. One Sunday evening after church, they decided to take me to see my dad. What they didn't know was that I had been rehearsing a speech for my dad. I felt that he was hanging on because he was worried about how we would survive without him. I had never had any real conversations with my dad. I do know that he and I had talked more than he did with any of my siblings. I started helping him with construction jobs when I was 12 years old. On weekends and during the summer, I would go and be his laborer. He was always so quiet. I think I literally jumped the first time he started to talk to me.

I learned that he had quit school and joined the Navy. I never found out where he learned his carpentry skills, but he could build anything! He taught me about work ethics and told me to try to be the first to start work and the last to stop. That lesson alone has made a HUGE difference in my life. So, two things I inherited from my dad: his work ethic, and unfortunately, his temper.

So, the youth group took me to the hospital. Since he was in ICU, only family visitors were allowed. They waited for me as I walked down the hall to see him. When I stepped in the room, his bed was directly across from the door. Two nurses on duty both gave me sympathetic smiles when I walked over to him. Even with all my rehearsing, I stood there unable to speak. Calm down! You can do this! You HAVE to do this! That little voice in my head was trying to encourage me. After a few minutes, I realized I could do this if I didn't look at his face. I picked up his hand and sat it in mine. I placed my other hand on top, took a long, deep breath, and started talking. It went something like this:

You have never said "I love you" to me, but I've always known. I realize I've never told you "I love you", but I'm telling you now. Tears that I had been fighting started rolling down my cheeks. I let them go. All the times that I had wanted or needed to let them out, but I had fought it. Now they poured out.

Then I said:

"I think you are hanging on because you are worried about us. I also think you are in pain. I want you to know that we will be okay. We will miss you, but we will make it. If you are holding on just for us, I want you to let go".

I let go of his hand and stepped back. Both nurses had moved in behind me and both had tears in their eyes. They had their arms on my shoulders when one of them said, "Oh my God! Look!" My dad's eyes were partially open. He was looking at me and his eyes were full of tears! No amount of medical explanation can change my mind. My dad heard my words and was telling me goodbye. And I love you.

I made my way back to the waiting room. My friends wrapped me up in the biggest group hug. Late the next afternoon, the vice-principal poked his head into my classroom and called me out into the hallway. The next day, the vice principal called me out of class. He told me my dad was dying and that if I hurried, maybe I could see him before it was too late. I dropped my books and I ran! I drove as fast as I could, breaking every moving violation in existence. It didn't matter. When I got there, he was gone. My dad was in the hospital for about 4 weeks. With that much time, you would think I would be prepared for this day, but I wasn't. I felt like I had aged years in that time span.

Life had forced me to grow up overnight.

We had his funeral in the small church I grew up in. I couldn't really tell you anything about the service, but I do remember this; two of the firefighters that answered the call to help my dad came to his funeral.

I sat the tombstone on my dad's grave. My friend Jeff and I formed up and poured a concrete curb around the double lot. My mom is there with him now. The gentleman that sold my mom the tombstone was the next person that God brought into my life.

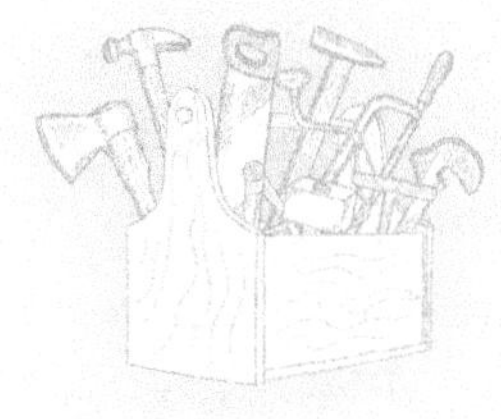

Tombstones
and Tote-The-Note

One morning a few weeks after the funeral, A man named John knocked on our door. My mom answered and I came to see who it was. I should have been in school, but lately, I missed more days than I attended. John had obviously read the obituary on my dad because he began telling my mom all the similarities he shared with her and my dad. I watched her face light up when John said he was from Georgia, just like my dad. John said he had relatives in Arkansas (where my mom was from). I think I see now where I inherited the naive part of my personality. As I sat and listened to his sales pitch, he kept checking me out, head to toe. Not in a perverted way, just sizing me up. John asked what I did for work, and before I could answer, my mom said that I had worked construction with my dad since I was 12. Now John had two objectives; to sell my mom a tombstone, and to offer me a job setting tombstones. He gave me directions to his office and asked me to come by the next day and see if this was something I would be interested in.

I drove to the address he gave me early the next morning. One half of the lot was an arrangement of tombstones. The other portion consisted of 10-12 used cars with the prices in shoe polish on the windshield. A small metal building served as the office. I found John inside, and I took a seat on an old couch by his desk. John offered me a drink before he noticed there was no coffee, and the little refrigerator was empty. He asked what I made at Red Lobster. I told him that it was about $3 an hour. With school and child labor laws, I would bring home $30-$40 dollars a week. John offered me $10 per hour, cash, and promised not to tell the IRS. I knew we desperately needed the money. I asked, "when can I start?" "How about now?" was his reply. While we were shaking hands, a man came in to make his weekly payment for his car. John thanked him, gave him a receipt, and after the man left, handed me $20. My first pay was for pulling weeds around the tombstones.

My first few days were spent helping the only other employee, Luke. Luke answered the office phone, set tombstones, and drank. Mostly the latter. As soon as John was convinced that I could handle setting a stone, he sent me out on my own. The granite tombstones were incredibly heavy, but Luke had shown me how to move them. We used the rubber rollers from old "wringer" style washing machines to get them close to their base or concrete pad, and then wrestled them into place. It was hard, heavy work, but it kept my mind occupied.

John had used all his upsell tactics to convince my mom to add all the extras to my dad's stone. In the center she had my dad's picture, and beneath that some of the carpenter's tools were sandblasted in. All these things were high priced, but like funeral home directors, John knew how vulnerable my mom was and took full advantage.

There weren't always stones to be set. Some days, I cut the grass and some days I helped Luke wash the cars or jump them off when needed. A man from the Carpenter's Local Union stopped by our house one evening. He asked my mom some questions about how long my dad had been with the union, how long since he had done any work and so on. I know that he took one look around our house, took pity on us, and added extra hours into my dad's record to make my mom eligible for an insurance payout from the union. For a short time afterward, I was able to keep part of my pay from John. I had started driving my dad's truck and it needed some mechanical work. I was able to have it repaired and I drove it for several years.

When my dad's tombstone came back ready to be set, I asked John if I could add some extra items and work them off. I asked him to tell me the price for all the things I wanted and that I would work for free until they were paid in full. He agreed. I was able to pay for a separate granite base under the stone, the curb around the lot that Jeff and I had poured, and a pair of granite vases, one for each end of the base. Things we never could have afforded without the "sweat equity" agreement.

John had come along at a time when my number one priority was making money, not attending Science or English classes. When I had worked long enough to pay off all the extra items, John disagreed. He said I still owed him hundreds of dollars. Without my dad to back me up, I turned to the only one in my family that I knew would help. My big sister. I could write for days about her and still not cover everything. All I know about this episode is this, after she called John, he called later and said that we were even, and would I please drop the keys to the work truck off to Luke as soon as I could. I think you can learn from people, whether they are good or bad. I know that John was a salesman, nothing more. I had listened to him on the office phone giving grieving people the same sales pitch he had used on my mom, just changing the place he was born to fit the obituary he was reading.

Next was a real wake up call. My school counselor advised me that I would need more credits to graduate. I had to really bear down my senior year, but not before I had tried other options. With my mom's signature on my paperwork, I met with a recruiter from the Marine Corp. It felt like I was going against the grain. I still felt determined to be a firefighter. I still lifted weights and ran every day. I intended to drop out of school and join the Marines. I kept trying to convince myself that this decision had worked out okay for my dad, so it should be good enough for me.

The Induction Center

The ride to the Dallas Induction Center was eerily quiet. Two more guys had met us at the recruiter's office. I noticed how they grinned when they saw me. Both guys were big, over 6 feet tall, and 210-225 pounds. With the absence of conversation, I was unable to ignore that small voice inside my head. Was this the right decision for me? Did this help me with my ultimate goal of becoming a firefighter?

When we arrived, the recruiter walked us in and got us signed up. I'm guessing there were close to 100 men there that morning. I was by far the smallest one there.

We were split into groups, and my group went in to take the written portion of this process. Those of us that passed this part went in to begin our physical. Now came real intimidation. There were probably 12-15 left in my group. We were told to strip and stand shoulder to shoulder. The doctor made his way down the line. Starting at your head, he quickly checked your eyes, the glands in your neck, had you stick out your tongue and say ah. If any major scars or anything caught his attention, he would ask about it. There was an attendant with him taking down all the notes. The physical ended with the infamous," turn your head and cough." The attendant came into the next room and called out several names. Those called were told to go back in and see the doctor. The rest of us were told to take a seat and wait for our name to be called.

There was an older Marine sitting at a desk in the front of the room. I guess he was the gatekeeper. When he looked us over, he paused when he got to me. He held eye contact for a few seconds and then moved on. He told us that we were going to be called in one at a time to meet with some officers and answer some questions. We would also be allowed to ask any questions we might have.

As the names were called, the guys went into the next room. After that was done, I believe they went to lunch. When my group was down to the last 2 or 3, the Marine called me up to his desk. He was gruff looking, and I expected the "drill instructor" persona. Instead, he spoke to me more like a grandfather. He asked how old I was, and when I said 16, he visibly winced. He asked who had signed the form for me to be there. "My mom, sir." He asked what my dad thought of the idea, and I explained that he had recently died. When he asked why I wanted to be a Marine, I rambled about not liking school, needing to make more money, and my desire to become a firefighter when I got out of the military. I finally quit talking when I told him that I wanted to be an MP.

His demeanor softened even more. "Son, they aren't going to let a 16-year-old be an MP!" He asked what my recruiter had told me. I answered that all we had discussed was me becoming an MP. I gathered that he was not a big fan of some of the recruiters. He told me to ask the board members in the next room about my choices. He advised me to stick to my plan and went on to say that if I didn't agree with what they told me, DO NOT get sworn in.

I went back to my seat. I was the last one called in for the board. I answered all their general questions, but now, that voice inside my head was screaming at me! I remember wishing that my dad, or at least my big sister, was there to help me. I was still that shy kid I had always been. With no one there to speak for me, the voice was now more of a whisper, "You can do this. Tell them you do not want to be sworn in." The words came out of my mouth. My heart was pounding in my ears. They spent a few minutes trying to convince me that I should proceed to the swearing in portion. I stood up, pushed my chair back in and said, "No thank you." I think that was the first time I had ever stood up for myself. I was nervous going through it, but so relieved to have done so.

The older Marine gave me a bus token for my ride home. The recruiter called my house for at least the next week. Once he stopped calling, I was able to reaffirm my commitment to becoming a firefighter. I often wondered what would have happened if that Marine had not spoken to me? Where would I be today? Was he another one used to keep me on my way?

I knuckled down for school. I turned 17 before I started my senior year. My friend, Jeff, and I signed up for a class called "Outdoor Education." It was camping, canoeing, archery, trap and skeet, and so on. Early on, our teacher planned a canoe trip on the Brazos, with an overnight camp out. Jeff and I were talking about it when two girls asked us to be their partners. Melinda and Susan. This was a huge surprise because I liked Melinda! Things were looking up until Susan said she would be with me, and Melinda would be with Jeff. Oh well.

After that trip, we started dating. I got along well with her parents and her younger brother. A little while before graduation, she told me she was pregnant. Good thing her parents liked me! Susan was a junior, so she stayed out of the first half of her senior year, we were married by a Justice of the Peace just three weeks after my 18th birthday. We moved into a rented house a block away from my mom's house.

A lady at our church helped me get a job at Lone Star Gas Company. I was a meter reader. It was a full-time job with benefits. One weekend, my obviously pregnant wife and I were grocery shopping. Pretty tight budget, so everything I put in the basket, she took out. A man walked past our aisle, then stopped and came back. He started walking toward me. I could never have imagined how much this man would change my life.

Mike and the
Moving Company

The man walking up to us stopped in front of me. He asked if I had ever moved any furniture. I said, "no sir." He told me that he was in a bind. He had a truck full of furniture in the parking lot, but no one to help him unload it. He offered to pay me cash and bring me home when we were done. I agreed to help him. As we walked outside, I couldn't help but notice all the other men in the store and even in the parking lot that he could have asked for help.

When we got to his truck, he unlocked my door. As I scooted across the seat to unlock his, I saw a windshield sticker for the Fort Worth Fire Department. He must have thought I was on drugs when he climbed inside. I introduced myself, shook his hand like I was possessed, and started asking rapid fire questions about the fire department. He told me his name was Mike, and yes, he works for the FWFD. As we drove away from the store, he patiently answered all my questions. The first thing I asked was, how do I apply? Mike said for me to go to City Hall and ask for a "pink card" for the Fire Dept. Mike said address it to yourself, and when they are taking applications, the city will mail it out to you. Finally, I had the info I needed to really get started!

When we arrived at the house to unload, Mike spent a few minutes showing me how to lift with my legs, and how to carry the furniture carefully through the house. My dad had instilled in me the work ethic I needed to work hard. I really wanted to impress Mike!

We quickly and carefully unloaded the truck. The customer paid Mike in cash and even gave him a tip. Once we were back in the truck, Mike gave me $20 for working, and another $10 for half of the tip. It had only taken about 2 hours to unload the truck. I had made $30 for two hours effort at a time when minimum wage was less than $4 per hour. Even more important to me, I now knew how to apply for my dream job!

As we drove to my house, Mike asked where I worked now. I told him about my job at Lone Star Gas. Mike said he could really use someone like me on weekends or whenever you have time. He said, "If you will work with me whenever you can, I will do everything I can to help you get on the FWFD. A chance encounter in a grocery store, a chance to make a little extra money, and, oh yeah, the guy just happens to be a Fort Worth Firefighter! You can say "coincidence", but to me it was answered prayers. My feet did not touch the ground for days! God is good!

All the time! And, All the time, God is Good!

Needless to say, I was at City Hall on Monday after working with Mike.

I've never been accused of being patient. I checked the mail every day for that little pink card. I may even be guilty of grumbling and complaining about it not being there. An opportunity at Lone Star Gas came up that would move me to the service department. It paid a little more and offered me a chance to learn a skillset. I requested a transfer, and it was approved. For two weeks, I rode out with different guys in that department. When my two weeks were up, my new boss sat me down and told me that my new shift would be midnight to 8 am. I would be on this night shift until a day spot opened up. My friend Mike loved the schedule change! This made me available much more often. Most of Mike's helpers were off duty firefighters, and their schedules sometimes caused a conflict. My only problem now was getting enough sleep to be useful to anyone.

Since most of Mike's helpers were firefighters, they soon learned that anytime they worked with me, they should expect to be bombarded with questions. I will brag about them and say they all treated me like a kid brother. The more time I spent around them, the more certain I became that I really wanted to be a firefighter.

Even though the guys were from all different backgrounds, had different personalities, and all had their own likes and dislikes, they all seemed to share a passion for helping people. All these guys spoke about feeling a "calling" to the job. Not just seeing a "Help Wanted" sign or attending a Job Fair and deciding to try it. Don't get me wrong, there are some that come along that way, get lucky enough to get on, but they never seem to grasp the enormity of the privilege they are blessed with. It takes a "servants' heart". People entrust you with their lives, the lives of their children. Banks and businesses trust you with keys to their buildings. Trust like that has been earned and should never be taken for granted.

So, one day my card did come. I couldn't believe it! My first call was to Mike. I went to City Hall the next morning to fill out my formal application. I was scheduled for the entrance exam. It was really happening! I got scheduled for my test, and I knew I was on my way. Maybe.

Test Day

We were seated 2 per table. Test papers were passed out and instructions were given. You had 2 hours to pass the multiple-choice test. When they finally said, "You may begin", I was off like a shot. I finished with a lot of time left on the clock, turned in my test, and waited in the hallway. We had been assigned a number on our test. The grades were posted on the board next to that number. All of us crowded around, looking for our number. Mike had explained that just passing was not usually good enough. The highest grades were scheduled for a physical agility test. The lower passing grades had to wait and see how many of those higher scores passed the physical. Please God! Let me be a high number!

I pushed my way to the front, scanning the board looking for my number. That can't be right! Not only was my number not one of the highest, but I had also failed the written test. Upset. Depressed. Nothing could have prepared me for this outcome. I drove home. Then I called Mike.

I felt awful and I felt like I had let Mike down. Mike's response was so calm. "Don't worry about it. Fill out another card and take the next one. "You need to get a look at your test and see what happened". Mike hung up and called the administrative secretary at the Training Academy. He asked her if I could see my test. I think the question caught her off guard. She promised to ask if it was even possible. Mike called me back and told me to go there early the next morning and introduce myself.

I met her the next morning. She said the test administrator was supposed to pick up all the testing supplies. She tried calling his office, No answer. I know I've mentioned my lack of patience, so, after waiting all morning (probably 15 minutes}, I asked her to please try again. Still no answer. She tried a third time out of pity, and let it ring forever. I was losing hope. I decided to leave.

Walking back to my truck, all the negative comments from my mom were going through my mind. I usually turned any of her negatives into motivation, but this time I thought maybe she's right.

Reaching my truck, I heard someone calling my name. "He's here! He's here!" I met her halfway, she told me we would only be there long enough to gather all his materials, so I had better hurry!

He was in the room where we had taken our test. He was putting his things in his briefcase. I believe he could see how desperate I was. He found my answer sheet and gave me a copy of the test.

The first part of the test may be hard for me to explain:

The left column had letters like A-M. The right column had numbers 1-13. A line ran from a letter on the left to a number on the right. You followed the line from start to finish and ended up at the answer. I know he saw the confusion on my face. He came over to look at my test and instantly saw how I had made a mistake. Every answer was wrong. When the line I was following intersected another line, I picked the line that got me to the closest number. After seeing how I had messed up, I felt a renewed sense of direction. As soon as I got home, I called Mike.

The next weekday, I filled out another Pink Card. I kept up my running and lifting weights. My job moving furniture and climbing stairs helped make me stronger. My only real problem now was my schedule kept me from getting enough sleep. My lack of sleep reached a breaking point one night.

Toward the end of my shift at Lone Star Gas, I was leaving a service call around TCU in Fort Worth. I pulled to a 4-Way stop. I woke up sometime later, still at the stop sign, my foot still on the brake. I have no idea how long I was there. The dispatcher had called me on the radio to check on me. Otherwise, I might have slept until cars started honking. Once again, God took care of me. I got my next Pink Card later that week.

Mike had stressed the importance of not just passing the written test but getting one of the highest scores. The highest scores were the first ones scheduled for the physical agility test. I believe I was physically prepared for the first test, now I felt mentally prepared as well.

I passed the exam! Not only that, I had one of the higher scores! I was told someone would contact me with a day/ time for the physical agility portion. So, this time with good news, I called Mike!

Later that next week, Mike asked me to come by his station. He and a couple of firefighters from his station were going to show me a few of the most difficult portions of the physical. When I go there, they took out a 2 ½ inch firehose and a big nozzle out to the street. They hooked the hose to the hydrant and turned on the water. They stretched it out straight, right along the curb. Two of the SO-foot sections, full of water, and under pressure, probably weighed as much as I did!

They put me in a bunker coat and 2 of them lifted the hose onto my shoulder. They told me to lean forward, lock my arms on the nozzle, and get ready. When they said go, I was supposed to swing wide left to the other side of the street and run with the hose until the first coupling passed the hydrant. "Whatever you do, DON'T STOP MOVING YOUR FEET!" If my memory serves me correctly, you have 30 seconds to complete this evolution.

Swinging wide and crossing the street was hard enough! When you first turn back, and the hose makes a big "C", it's like pulling a truck! I was in shape for most things, but I had never experienced anything like this. Leaning so far forward, and keeping my legs pumping, I made it! I'm not 100% sure I could have done it at the physical agility test if they had not shown me that I could do it. I was so ready!

Let's Do This!

I reported to the Training Academy and started checking out the other applicants. Almost all these guys were big, maybe construction workers, or athletes in high school or college. I wasn't surprised to be the smallest one there. I believe there is a fine line between being really confident and being cocky. I hoped they could tell I was confident.

Every event is timed, and all are pass/fail. We started with a 1 ½ mile run, and some of the big guys didn't make it in the allotted time. By the time we were at the hose drag, there were only about a dozen of us left. Guys were cramping up and losing their breakfast all around. I slipped for just a second when they sat the hose on my shoulder. A couple of the guys snickered. That was all the motivation I needed! I passed everything! We were congratulated and told that we would be contacted about when to meet with the polygraph examiner, and to be prepared to answer questions from our background investigator. I had waited years for this opportunity, and it was finally happening! I get goosebumps writing this part and remembering how incredible it felt.

Of course, like always, when I got home, I called Mike. One More Surprise Later the next week, I got a letter from the city. I remember thinking it's the time and place for the polygraph, or it's the background investigator setting a schedule. I started reading.

We regret to inform you of your disqualification for the position of Fire Trainee for the City of Fort Worth.

Reason for disqualification: Color Blindness

I was speechless. I remember taking the color blindness test, but the lady had just tried on 3 different pages and then sent me on to finish my eye exam. If you have never had a "colorblindness" test, the tester opens a spiral bound booklet and you see a big circle, full of different colored "bubbles". One color of the bubbles makes a number. When the lady opened the booklet, she asked, "what number do you see?" I started looking at all the little bubbles, believing that one of them had a number inside. I guess she could tell that I'm not seeing a number, so she flips the key to cover all the "extra" bubbles. There, plain as day, is a big number. Of course, now I can see it. When she removes the key, I lose it again.

Self-doubt is the worst. Once again, I started thinking maybe my mom was right. "You're too little. You're not as smart as you think you are." The more venomous ones, "You should have just joined the military and stayed until you could retire." Or my least favorite," You will never amount to anything. You're just like your dad". Usually, I could turn these phrases into pure motivation. They would usually drive me to accomplish whatever I needed, just to prove her wrong. I'm not going to lie, this setback hurt the most. I was already convinced that I would be in the next class. Now, I didn't know if I would ever see this dream come true.

I called Mike.

Mike's Friend, Chief Cox

Mike never got discouraged with all the obstacles. He had a way of re-assuring me that this was just a speedbump. Another hurdle. Later that evening, Mike called me back. He told me to go to the Public Safety Building and meet Deputy Fire Chief Cox tomorrow morning.

I remember not letting myself get hopeful or excited. When I walked into the main office, I started to get nervous. My palms were sweaty, and my voice started cracking. I have never been comfortable speaking, especially to someone I don't know. Compound that with this man's position, now I was a basket case.

Have you ever met someone that you could instantly tell they are a good person, that they have a good heart? It seems strange now, but I remember thinking how his kind eyes reminded me of Capt. Hunter, our original angel.

Chief Cox had me sit down and we just talked. I know he could tell I was nervous, so the conversation was to put me at ease He said," I heard you may be colorblind?" I said, "Yes sir." He told me, "Let's see". He laid a piece of yarn on his desk. The top of the desk was solid black, and with that background, I had a much better result. Anytime I struggled or paused, Chief Cox would say, "Is this one blue?" "Yes Sir!" His smile told me it was safe to say yes. He called me over to the office window. "What color is the traffic light?" I answered Green. "Ok, how about now?" I answered yellow. "And, what about now?" I said red. The Chief said, "You're not colorblind! You were just confused!"

He put his arm around my shoulder and told me that he and Mike had been good friends for a long time. He said that when Mike called about me, he couldn't remember Mike ever calling on behalf of anyone else. He said," Mike believes in you, and he believes you will be a great firefighter, and so do I. Mike doesn't lie".

Mike believing in me, and always encouraging me, changed my life. I will forever be indebted to him, and I've tried to help other people that sought this occupation, especially if they seemed to have been "called."

Before I left the Chief's office, I thanked him profusely! He said that he had one favor to ask. "Anything, Sir" He said," Please never try out for the Bomb Squad. Those guys have to know what color wire to cut."

Chief Cox asked his secretary to please call the Training Academy and request them to enroll me in the upcoming class. Hallelujah!!

You remember me talking about Walter? The very end of his prayers always closed this way.

"And we give Thee all the Praise. In Jesus' name we pray, Amen."

Maybe that is what had been holding me back all this time. I had prayed for it, worked for it, Mike had gone above and beyond to help, but I had so many hurdles and heartbreaks along the way. Maybe it's because I forgot to give Him all the praise! The opening line of the Doxology goes.

"Praise God from whom all blessings flow" Thank you, God! I give you all the Praise!

The Early Years

My mom told me that when I was born, we lived in a small house on the Southside of Fort Worth. Years later, I would spend a large part of my career as a Fire Captain just a few blocks from that house.

My first memories were from a small house in Acton, where the Pecan Plantation subdivision now sits. Mostly I remember my best friend, my babysitter, and my protector, George.

George was a beautiful collie that to me looked just like Lassie. George went everywhere with me. He kept me out of trouble and would not let me get too far from the house. He always knew when the school bus was bringing my big sister home. We would walk up to the gate and wait for her.

My dad took care of the property owner's cows. George kept me away from the cows, or they away from me. He was my first best friend.

One morning when I got up, I started calling his name. I didn't see him anywhere. I went outside looking all around. My sister came outside crying. She said George had been hit by a car and had died. I was heartbroken! It has been over 60 years since he died. I still think about him and still miss him.

We moved a couple of times before we ended up on the West side of Fort Worth. It was the house I grew up in. It was where we lived when my dad died, and where my mom lived until she died. It was a small house, but it always seemed bigger to me as a kid. Three bedrooms, one bath for two adults and four kids.

When my mom died, my younger sister and I were getting things out of the house to put it up for sale. Every room held lots of memories. Some good, some bad. For a number of years, my little brother lived there with my mom. They were very dependent on each other. If you saw them together, you would think they looked like an old married couple.

They had their share of disagreements. My mom was not easy to get along with. At least, that's my opinion of her. My brother had his own demons that he dealt with. Don had never married, and I don't remember him ever having a serious girlfriend. He was always one of the "March to the beat of a different drummer" kind of people, for as far back as I can remember. He and my little sister, Barbara, were the closest in age, and maybe the closest of all the siblings. Don has mental health issues and lives in a nursing home. Barbara is his caretaker, and definitely his advocate.

Don and I shared a bedroom growing up, but we were never close. I will go see him when Barbara and her husband come for a visit. I'm not 100% sure he knows who I am. I don't dislike him, but I do feel sorry for him. In my opinion, some of his mental problems are hereditary, but some are self-inflicted.

We were polar opposites growing up. I tried so hard to be the "good kid." I got good grades. I liked sports, and I had some friends. Don started smoking at a young age. He tried dipping snuff. I don't remember anyone that you would label as 'friends." Any of the people he hung around with all seemed to live on the fringe of society. I believe they bonded together because they shared the same ideology. Looking back, I believe Don was the most affected by losing my dad. He was only 13 at the time. I also believe that he lost his final anchor when my mom died.

My mom was extremely hardheaded, very opinionated, and could definitely be mean. She grew up in rural Arkansas on a farm. I believe they struggled daily. She had no filter. Whatever thought popped into her head spewed out of her mouth. No regard for anyone's feelings or beliefs. If anyone pointed out that what she said may be hurtful or insensitive, you would hear one of her most famous sayings; "If they don't like it, they can lump it!" Whatever the Hell that means.

I'm not speaking ill of the dead. She wore these parts of her personality with a badge of honor. I could write a series of Time Life books about her, and never adequately describe the way she was. Rant over for now.

After my dad died, Don's downward spiral accelerated. He started smoking pot and skipping school. Each year got worse. He was arrested for theft and spent a couple days in jail. As much as I hated to, I took my mom to pick him up.

After I had gotten married, my mom called almost daily, complaining that she couldn't control him. She would beg me to come over and talk to him. If I did give in and go there, she wouldn't let me inside the house. Probably a good thing.

I was running on empty. Working at the gas company and moving furniture was like two full-time jobs. Add in my workouts, and my fuse was even shorter than normal. So, it was one of those days that my mom called. Again. I hung up and drove to her house. This time I just remained in my truck. I could see her looking out of the window, but I stayed put. Finally, she couldn't stand it. She came outside and approached my truck. I motioned for her to come around to my side. When she reached the back of the truck, I bolted for the door. I knew I could beat her inside. I locked the door behind me.

Don was laying on the couch facing away from me. He said, "What did that son of-a b****want?" I told him that I came to offer him two options. Option 1, you go tomorrow and join the Army. Option 2, I drag you off the couch and kick your sorry a**! My mom always said he spent all day smoking and watching old westerns. He must have thought that he shared some of the toughness and bravery of his cowboy heroes. He picked option 2.

A minute or so later, he decided to join the Army. Unless he told my mom what had transpired while she tried to get back inside, she never knew. She did stop calling me for a long time. Finally!

After he completed his basic training, he went to Germany. I'm not sure what he was taking now, but he came back even more screwed up than when he left. My persuasive skills would be called upon again when he "volunteered" to go to a 30- day rehab for his addiction.

Not only do I think my dad's death had the most negative impact on Don, I think he started really acting out to gain my mom's attention. My little sister was only 12 when my dad passed away, but she adjusted in a much more mature manner. Maybe it was just them dealing with grief in their own way. I still believe Don would not have acted this way if my dad were still alive.

For the last several years of her life, my mom's sole reason for living was taking care of Don, she knew that he needed help, but she became the biggest enabler of his life. They were so dependent on each other. I thought that when one of them died, the other would go shortly thereafter. I said earlier that Don now lives in a Nursing home, but the word, "lives" is questionable. I think it's more true to say," he exists."

He receives great care at this home. A thousand times better than the first place he went. He lays in bed most of the day, watching IV, and sleeping. He lost his dentures at the first home and is on a pureed food diet. He has to be closely watched. He has been stealing food from the other patients and has aspirated a couple of times.

He complains of a constant hunger. Maybe the term, "exists" is also a misnomer. On a positive note, Don suffered a fall at the first home. He got subdural hematoma. It apparently took away his remembrance of being a chain smoker. The physician said the injury may have affected his brain. Maybe the portion of his brain that signals when you are full is non-operational.

I don't feel like we were dysfunctional. I believe we adapted our lifestyle to fit our situation. Play the hand you're dealt. I'm certain that most of the time we qualified for food stamps or welfare. My dad's pride kept us from even applying. He took the responsibility of providing for his family very seriously. I also believe the stress he endured trying to keep a roof over our heads and food on the table, put him in an early grave. And I don't think my mom's almost daily nagging and complaining made his life any easier. They never appeared to be a team. I never saw them really happy. I always hated the way my dad never got to enjoy the fruits of his labor. He loved to hunt and fish, but I can count on one hand the times he got to go.

I saw the biggest change in my dad when my big sister, Brenda, had a baby. They lived right across the street for a while, so we saw them all the time. No matter how tired my dad was from working, seeing his grandson brought the biggest smile to his face. To be 100% honest, it made me jealous. My mom even commented on his behavior. She said that he was never like that with us, not even when we were babies. As soon as my sister would bring him over, my dad would carry him around with a big smile on his face. Somewhere, there are pictures of my dad with David Jr., and both are smiling. David Jr. was too young when my dad passed away to remember him. Shortly after my dad's funeral, Brenda blamed my mom for my dad's heart attack. Brenda is at least as hardheaded as my mom, and she severed all ties with my mom from that day forward. My brother-in-law, David Sr., tried in vain to get my sister to patch things up with my mom. He made sure my mom got to see both grandsons, and when the boys got older, they stayed in contact with her. Brenda never relented on her vow to never speak to her again. Actually, I was a little surprised to see her at my mom's funeral. I know she regrets her decision to stay away from my mom, and to never speak to her again.

Both of Brenda's sons were pallbearers at my mom's funeral.

During my mom's last days, she often thought that Barbara was, in fact, Brenda. She talked about my dad being in the room with her, and about talking to her mom and dad. My mom passed away from Alzheimer's and was buried on my birthday. She was buried in the cemetery in Acton, next to my dad. She had been without him for over 45 years, I would love to have seen that reunion. For both of them.

When I first thought of writing this story, I never realized how therapeutic it could be. I also never dreamed it could be so emotional. Like picking at a scab, things you thought were long since healed are reopened, and you find they have strong feelings still attached. Just writing about my dad brings all those feelings to the forefront. If the love you have for a dog, that's been gone so long, still makes you sad, imagine the feelings connected when the one lost is your family, or a close friend. For me, it's a hollow feeling. It's an ache that is always in the back of your mind. Whether the memories are good or bad, there is still a void. I guess you can rejoice that your family, your friends, and even your dog, were a part of your life. And, they will always have a special place in your heart.

Training Days

The last step to being a candidate for the Fire Trainee position in the Training Academy is the Review Board. Five of the senior officers in the department had the chance to ask you questions, and to go over any concerns noted on the polygraph or background check. My biggest fear is now, and probably always will be, any type of public speaking.

The review started with the general questions; how old you are, where did you go to school, and so on. I wanted this job so badly, but I was still reluctant to give more than short answers. Then came the time when I had to talk! The question was," Why do you want to be a firefighter?" I took a big, deep breath and started. I told them the same story I shared with you earlier. I told them about the firefighters taking care of my dad. I talked about Capt. Hunter, the care package, and the money. I ended my little spiel telling them about some of the firefighters coming to my dad's funeral.

The temperature in the room warmed instantly. These officers were all touched to hear how those firefighters had made such an impact on my family. If they previously had any doubts about my qualifications, especially with all the difficulties I faced just to get this far, they never expressed them. One of the chiefs walked me out. In now what I believe is a common gesture, he put his arm around my shoulder, looked me in the eye and smiled. "You're in. Congratulations!"

It had definitely taken longer than I thought it would. Maybe it was God's way of making sure I could handle it. Either way, I believe with all my heart, and all my soul, that it was God's will all along. It was supposed to happen when it did, not just when I wanted it. Looking back, I see all the obstacles were tests of faith.

Every time I felt defeated, every time I felt like a failure, the answers appeared before me. Whether they found me in a grocery store or sat beside me explaining test questions. They always showed up. I thank God for putting all those people in my life, and always just when I needed them. What may seem like random meetings, or "coincidences", are highlighted in my mind. To me, they are answered prayers. Thank you, God!

Day 1

Our training instructors introduced themselves to the class. They explained what was expected of us, and what our training would consist of. It was July 20th, 1978. In order to successfully complete our training and graduate, we had to pass all our courses. We were going to be taught Fire Science, Hydraulics, and basic First aid. We were observed during hose evolutions and live fire training. We had Physical Fitness training every day. And we bonded.

Almost all the firefighters I know are naturally competitive. Some, extremely so. You wanted to be the best, whether it was a written test, or a volleyball game. The instructors built our trust in each other, even while working to bring out the best in us individually.

The other side of the training academy was for the police trainees. Now, I'm not making fun of or belittling the police. I have the utmost respect for what they do. Especially these days! But every time we competed against their rookies, we dominated! Years later, I had been studying for a promotional exam. The competition was fierce! I saw the gentleman responsible for making these tests for both Fire and Police.

I asked him how difficult it was to come up with the test questions. He said," For the firefighters, it's extremely difficult! I could ask for the barcode inside the cover of the book and some of them would know it. For the police, I could ask their name, phone number, and address, and I'm not surprised if they miss 2 of the 3!" His words, not mine!

All joking aside, there is a tremendous amount of respect between both professions. Scene safety is paramount, whether at a fire, vehicle accident, or a medical call. We relied completely on the police officers to have our back.

I pray for the men and women that risk their lives to protect us. It seems like a lot of people have lost sight of what they endure. I know that some have no business in that profession. The same can be said for any profession. Bad firefighters, bad bankers, bad teachers, and don't even get me started on bad politicians! They are all human. Well, maybe not the politicians! Seriously, most of us don't know all they go through on a shift. Disrespected, cursed, even assaulted. A lot have been killed just doing their job. I support them and respect them for devoting their lives to protecting others, I can't even imagine what our lives would be like without them. I hope I never have to find out.

I was 19 when our Academy class started, I turned 20 less than 2 weeks later. The days and weeks flew by. We soon started preparing for our Academy Final, followed closely by the Civil Service Test. I had never been good at taking home my books during school. I did most of my homework at lunch, or even in the mornings before class. I was fortunate. I got good grades, at least in the beginning, by paying attention in class. I had a decent ability to retain what I heard. After my dad died, I paid less and less attention, and my grades reflected that fact. I attacked the Academy courses and tests included like a man possessed!

The instructors set junk cars on fire. They started fires in the drill tower using hay bales and wooden pallets. We climbed ladders, and we pulled hose. We cleaned everything. We learned basic First Aid from the American Red Cross. And we bonded.

If you ever see firefighters smile when they come out of a burning building, it's usually from the adrenaline rush. They aren't smiling or laughing because of someone's loss. Just think of this: The firefighters pull up in front of a house on fire. Everyone inside is running out. Rats and roaches know to leave. Now, the firefighters are running inside. It's a HUGE adrenaline rush! If the fire is one that allows an "offensive" attack, it's an even bigger thrill. Look at the title they wear Firefighter! The job is dangerous, and you can get hurt. Some even die. It takes aggression, but "controlled" aggression. You seldom hear a lot of yelling on the scene. I heard a citizen once say," It's like watching a symphony. Everyone knows their job, their part to play, and they just do it."

The atmosphere speeds up anytime there is a possibility that people may still be inside. The firefighters know that the most valuable thing inside that building is the trapped people. All life is precious. Houses and furnishings can be replaced. "Things "are expendable. Replaceable. You should never see a smile at one of these type calls.

The "weight" of a loss of life is taken back to the station by all involved. With any luck, they talk about it, and start dealing with it as a group. Some of the best therapy sessions are held around the table with a cup of coffee. Talking about what just happened is like a pressure relief valve. It's important for your mental health to not carry those things around with you, and not to have them building up in your mind.

You see things you wish you could "unsee." Pursuing this type of work puts you in a position to see people suffering, physically and mentally. Horrific injuries leave horrific images in your head. Calls involving children are especially stressful. That stress can be compounded if you have children of your own. These type calls can make you hug and hold your own children tighter than normal. Telling a spouse or anyone else about the things you see may be a relief for you, but at what cost?

Never ask "What's the worst call you've ever made?" They don't need to relive that experience, and you probably don't really need to know.

One of the most rewarding parts of my job was the feeling you get from helping somebody. They are almost always happy to see you. You show up what may be one of the worst days of their life, and you do everything you know how to make it better. It's rewarding and fulfilling, the more you can help, the more satisfying it is! If you drive up, put out the fire, roll up the hose, pat them on the back, and leave, that's one thing. If, instead, you put out the fire, call any agency you know of that may be able to further assist them with things such as housing, food, clothing, etc. Help them with any of their belongings, such as phones, purses, keys, prescriptions, then you have thoroughly helped them. They will remember that help, and who provided it forever. You may be the only experience they ever have with a firefighter. Make sure you make a good impression. Perception is reality.

Graduation Day

I wish I could tell you about the inspirational speech given by our class president. All I really remember is wanting to get to a station. I felt like I knew everything I needed and could do anything asked of me. Well, I already told you I was very naive. All the weeks of training had not even scratched the surface of what I needed to know. I was about to embark on a lesson plan that would last over 34 years. You should learn something from each call. Sometimes, if you don't, it's because you aren't paying attention.

Sometimes, it seemed that everything I learned, I learned the hard way. A lot of the lessons from the Academy instructors had been from "lessons learned." Bad outcomes usually change behavior. Policy changes are usually from previous bad outcomes. People learn from their mistakes, and fire can be a very cruel teacher.

After we graduated, my first shift was Christmas Day! Best gift ever! I was told to report to Station 16. That station was the district headquarters for District 5. The districts were later changed to Battalions.

This meant that this was the Station where the Battalion Chief officed and responded from. So, the "official" shift change time was 8:00 am. We were taught that it was customary to go in around 7:00. When you arrived, if you were assigned to that station for that shift, you were told which apparatus to put your gear on. You would remove the gear from the firefighter that was going off-duty and put it in their locker. In those days, the shifts were 24/48. 24 hours on, then 48 hours off. If you worked at a busy station, your shift went by quickly, but then you needed some of your off time to recuperate. If you were at a slow station, 24 hours could seem like a prison sentence. I always preferred the busy stations. Complacency was a pitfall of some of the slower places.

Once the previous shift firefighter was relieved, we were taught to go thoroughly over every compartment of the trucks. Being able to go directly to the compartment for whatever you needed was very important. You needed to not only find the item you were sent for, but you also needed to know how to use it. We started the power tools regularly and made sure we always had fuel for them.

Over the years, I tried to never lose track of my "debt." We started a yearly practice of "adopting "a family for Christmas. We located a local family that might need help. Some of these were located by a response to their home, and some were recommended by local charities. At first, it was just our shift. Firefighters on the other two shifts, and even from other stations saw what we were doing and wanted to help. There was never a shortage of people needing help.

We would meet with the family and see what they needed most. We would get the clothing sizes for the kids, shoe sizes, and get the groceries needed for Christmas dinner. We would bring a tree and decorations. Sometimes there was a financial need that we could help with, such as paying a utility bill. Once, we bought a new microwave. If you want to see pure joy, try this with your church group, or even just your friends. I'm not sure who received the greatest blessing, the kids and their parents, or the firefighters!

Just my opinion, but, if this kind of experience that comes from helping others doesn't touch your heart, then you will never be happy in this profession.

Unfortunately, there will always be those who hear about what the firefighters are doing and try to take advantage. It only happened once with our station, but it ruined the experience for some of the firefighters; On Christmas morning, the trucks were loaded with toys and clothes, and they drove to the house. A lot of the background checking had not been completed, and the family said that they didn't need a tree, or groceries. When asked about clothes and toys, the list was not normal. Very expensive clothing and toys were requested. When the trucks pulled up to the house, it was very nice. There were 2 very expensive, new vehicles in the driveway. The firefighters were puzzled but thought there may be a logical explanation. When the parents saw the toys and clothes that were brought in, they were outraged! "That's not what we told you our kids wanted!" The firefighters were shocked. The parents were furious. The sad part is, somewhere, there was a family with little or nothing that morning, that would have been overjoyed to get those things. The other sad part is it turned some firefighters away from participating the next year.

During the school year, we started participating in the "Big Brother" program in our community. We found a contact for that organization and invited them to our station. We learned that there were way more kids that needed "big brothers" than there were people willing to fill that need. The kids and their parents would come by with the representative from the office. If there were no reservations from the parents, the kids would come by a couple of times a week after school. The kids usually had dinner with us. While they were there, a firefighter usually helped with their homework. I know that I have been saying "parents", but the truth was the kids were with single moms. We were lucky to have been big brothers to some awesome kids. Once again, I'm not sure who received the biggest blessing.

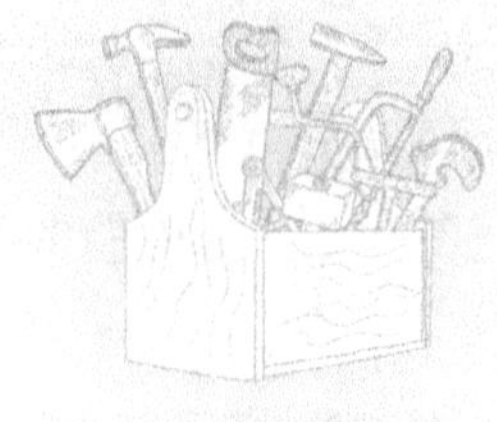

My First Fire

I was assigned to Station 16 just a few days after graduating from the Academy. A couple of weeks later, I would get my first fire. Sometime late that night, our tone went off for a "reported structure fire", and we were the first due engine! You could see the glow from the fire and smell the smoke before we arrived. My Lieutenant and the other firefighter started pulling the hose line, as I retrieved an SCBA (self-contained breathing apparatus) from the rear compartment on the engine. We had been trained to have our SCBA on in 30 seconds or less, so I quickly got to the nozzle. The side door was kicked open, and in I went. Unlike movies, or television shows, you can't usually see anything. We trained in blacked-out masks, so that wasn't a problem. About 2 steps inside the room, I took my first breath in that environment. My facepiece filled with thick, black smoke. I used the purge valve to let a blast of fresh air into my facepiece, but that just had me breathe in some smoke. I'm not too proud to tell you, I panicked. The Lieutenant and the other firefighter were at the door pulling slack for the hose. I held onto the nozzle, turned back to the door I came in, and bowled both guys over, trying to get outside in the fresh air. A quick inspection in the driveway found the problem. A small "O" ring was missing from the regulator! I grabbed another SCBA, put it on, and went back inside. The fire was out, no thanks to me, and now we were searching the rooms for anyone inside. I turned to my right and found a wall. Next to the wall was a baby bed. Feeling on the mattress, I felt a foot. Then a leg. Feeling for a head, I found out it was a doll. I received a lot of good-natured ribbing when we got back to our station, but one of the firefighters on the ladder truck told the guys to leave me alone. He said," He's the smallest guy here and he knocked you both on you're a** when he wanted out of there!"

I was almost always one of the first ones up. It reminded me of getting up when my dad would be eating breakfast before he left for work. I would just sit there watching him, and listening, just in case he talked. I would go back to bed after he left. At the station, I would make coffee, get the newspaper, and make sure no dishes were left in the sink. Believe it or not, you were judged as much on being a roommate, as you were on a fireground. You also would quickly learn that the dining table was also a place to prove yourself.

The kidding would start, aimed at anyone. The officers were fair game, even if some didn't like it. The barbs would be thrown around at anyone present and were usually fast paced. The bouncing would stop as soon as someone got "stung" and responded in anger. This caused a feeding frenzy! Rapid-fire barbs were thrown out and even redirected to the others. You had to learn to keep a even keel, and also learn to quickly send a better barb back to the original "offender"!

We picked on each other, but no one from another station could pick on any of our people. This whole dynamic filled a need in me that I didn't know existed. A sense of belonging. We treated each other like family. We basically lived with our brothers and sisters for a third of our career. We worked together, ate together, laughed and even cried together. Anyone from the outside looking in may not have seen or even believed it, but we cared deeply for each other.

My Home Away from Home

When we were younger, my friend Jeff lived a few blocks away. He and his mom moved away a few years and that's the only time I remember us not really keeping in touch. When they moved back, Jeff had a stepdad. They eventually moved close to the middle school we attended. I absolutely loved going to his house!

Jeff's mom, Twila, was a fantastic cook. I really loved her cooking, but I think the thing that kept me wanting to go back again and again, was the love you felt in that house. Twila always hugged me Hello and Goodbye. If you grew up in a similar situation, you might not appreciate it as much. If you didn't, then you craved it. You never wanted to leave. Jeff had an older stepbrother named Jack. Jack married a beautiful woman named Sharon. Now, when I went to their house on Sundays, Twila would hug me, Sharon, and even Joe and Jack would hug me. All the affection was intoxicating! Leaving after lunch was almost depressing.

Jeff and his whole family taught me so much. This is how families are supposed to be. Whatever your situation, be it financial, emotional, you name it, you are a team. You let all your family know that they are loved, that they are important to you. You treat your friends like family. I'm so thankful that Jeff's family were role models for me.

I promised myself that my kids would never question whether I loved them. I promised to be affectionate. I promised to be easy to talk to, and always be there for them. Turns out, it was not as easy as I thought. I wasn't as distant as my dad, or as cold as my mom, but I was far from being what I dreamed of being. Despite my shortcomings, there is a positive outcome. My son, Jason, is married to a beautiful young lady named Sunshine. That's the most appropriate name ever given! Sunshine has three beautiful daughters, and I can clearly see that Jason loves them deeply, and they return that love tenfold. I think it's so awesome when you can "see" that people love each other.

I have another child, a beautiful daughter. She and my oldest grandson, Greg, lived with us for a few years after she went through a divorce. Becky and my daughter could not seem to get along. Harsh words and hurt feelings took their toll. My daughter had always been a "daddy's girl" growing up. I believe she felt betrayed when I took Becky's side in one of their biggest arguments. I last spoke to her almost 10 years ago. I still miss her and love her very much. But I have made peace with her decision. My door is always open, and my arms are ready to hug her and hold her, but only when she's ready.

Jason was a pallbearer at my mom's funeral. My daughter didn't attend.

Spencer

When I was promoted to Captain, I was assigned to Station, in the Hospital District, on the south side of Fort Worth. We had an engine and a truck, and our staffing was 4 personnel on each. Most, if not all, of the firefighters assigned there, had more fire experience than I did. I consider this assignment at Station 8, to be where I received most of my "education." It was a busy station, and we answered with other busy stations. There was a certain comfort in that knowledge, knowing that neighboring stations would be there to assist you with whatever, as soon as humanly possible. Very aggressive firefighters were like the cavalry coming to help. It was a security blanket.

We had one practice that I never completely understood. The officers would rotate shifts. Captains went one way, Lieutenants, the other. With as much emphasis as there was on team building, the movement of anybody, especially your officers, seemed counterproductive. It wasn't until I had moved to another shift and had the chance to meet Spencer, that I really appreciated the opportunity.

Spencer was a firefighter, but he was so much more than that. I believe he had the quickest wit of anyone I've ever met. Spencer was a few years older than me and had been assigned to that station for several years before I got there. He was a wealth of knowledge and was a great teacher to all of us. I never saw him in a bad mood. We became quick friends and spent many shifts practicing our wit on each other.

Spencer was an incredible athlete. I'm sure that any sport he participated in, he mastered. One year, he decided to enter the Cowtown Marathon, a 26.2 mile run around parts of the city of Fort Worth. Spencer started training by running to the station on his shift. I don't even know how far it was, but that was his regimen from the start. Run to the station, work your shift, then run home. If he was tired or sore, I never heard him complain.

The day of the marathon was a shift day for us. Spencer had another firefighter work his shift that day. Sitting in my office early that afternoon, I got a call from another station. It went something like this; "Hello Gary, don't you have a guy at your station named Spencer?" Yes, I do. "Is he running the Cowtown today?" Yes sir. "You guys need to get to Harris Hospital. He collapsed at the finish line." That's impossible! "Some of our guys are working at the race, and they saw him collapse. You better hurry!"

I got on the PA system and told all the crew to meet me upfront. NOW. I relayed the message as quickly as I could, as we headed to the trucks. Harris Hospital was a stone's throw from our station, so we were there in a heartbeat. We parked the trucks by the Emergency entrance and ran inside. We saw some of the medics we normally responded to calls with, and the look on their faces told us all we needed to know.

We saw Spencer's wife talking with a doctor. The doctor took a couple of us back to Spencer. There is absolutely nothing I could have heard or seen at that time that would have prepared me for seeing Spencer like that. I had been working long enough to have seen more than my share of dead people. His vibrant spirit, his incredible sense of humor, his dedication to his family, and to his friends, all gone! Even his athletic body was not the same. I didn't want to see him this way, but I couldn't leave.

Other firefighters, our department Chaplain, and more family and friends came down. The hospital staff was so gracious to accommodate us. The only thing more painfully emotionally than seeing hard charging firefighters crying for their brother was seeing the ones that couldn't shed tears. You could see the raw pain on their faces. The look in their eyes shows up in my dreams, My nightmares.

The church was full to overflowing for Spencer's service. There was a large number of family and friends, but the largest portion of the mourners were made up of Spencer's other "family." The men and women in uniform sat or stood shoulder to shoulder They were there to pay their respects, to show support to Spencer's family, and to support each other. If you can find anything more emotional than a firefighter's funeral, I don't want to see it. It is one thing we certainly do right.

We were allowed the privilege of transporting Spencer's casket to his resting place at the cemetery. I didn't say his "final" resting place because I fully believe that Spencer is sitting in Heaven, entertaining the saints and angels with his quick wit, patiently waiting for his brothers and sisters to join him.

RIP brother. I love you. See you soon.

Our Fire Chief at that time nominated Spencer for the Rotary Club Man of the Year. I have mentioned several times that I'm not a speaker. I write the things I wish I could say. So, when our Chief asked if I would like to say something about Spencer, I declined. I asked him if I could write something for him to read instead. Thankfully he agreed.

The day of the Rotary Club meeting, I sat with Spencer's widow, and several members of the administration staff. Our chief was blessed with a "speaking voice." He could read the phone book to you and keep your attention. After the business meeting portion was over, the Rotary Club President spoke about the number of nominations received, and how difficult the decision had been. He said that one nomination stood out from the rest. Spencer was announced as the winner! Our Chief spoke in a reverential tone about Spencer, then said he had something from Spencer's Captain that he would like to read. I could feel my face flush, and even my ears turned red. I got sweaty palms, and my pulse pounded in my temples. I couldn't even look around the room. After he finished reading, a beautiful plaque and a check were presented to Spencer's wife and family. I believe that all the women and most of the men, were wiping tears from their eyes. It was the first time I had written anything that caused any reaction other than anger. All that I had done was sit down and think about Spencer, I know he would not have wanted any of this recognition. He would not have approved of me using any "sissy" words or phrases to describe him, or how much he meant to us. Sorry, brother, it just fit!

One scripture from the funeral was a perfect fit; 2 Timothy 4: 7-8. "I have fought the fight. I have finished the race" (NIV). Spencer had called out to his wife as he crossed the finish line and collapsed. He FINISHED, then collapsed. That was absolutely Spencer. Who knows how long he suffered, or how bad he felt. An aortic aneurysm had ended his life way too soon. Doctors told us that even if he were in the hospital when it happened, there would be nothing they could have done. The fact that he finished has motivated me on so many occasions. I still miss him.

I've crossed paths with so many people in my life. Most were good, but some were definitely bad. In my life, the good have always outnumbered the bad. I also have been blessed to work with some of the true, "salt of the earth people."

in this profession. I still believe people that gravitate to this type of work are "called" to it. No one has ever shared a similar experience with me about being convinced that everyone they meet is sent to help them reach this destination. A lot have followed in their family's footsteps. Some of my best friends come from a long line of firefighters. In my humble opinion, if you do not feel drawn to this job, you will never truly feel the incredible rewards from helping others.

I've had the opportunity to live and work with people with so much compassion, so much dedication, and a definite Servant's Heart. "Greater love hath no man than this, that a man lay down his life for his friends." John 15:13

Vince

I feel like I've been putting this one off because it's the most recent, or maybe because Vince wasn't a firefighter. But he was one in spirit. A phone call from a police officer changed my life and my outlook, so much more than I could ever imagine.

A little backstory: One of my best friends, David, was a Captain at Station 8 before I was assigned there. David had been my lieutenant at Station 18, where I drove the engine. Years later, a Captain's vacancy opened at Station 8, and I had recently passed that test. David convinced the other Captain that they should recruit me for that opening. (Surely by now you can see why I don't believe in coincidences!) The other Captain agreed, and it was approved. Sometime later, David had begun researching Thermal Imaging cameras for use in firefighting. The cameras were currently used by the military, and David was convinced that they could assist firefighters in locating hidden fire, and with finding victims. David recommended that the city purchase the cameras for the fire department. The assistant city manager at that time denied the request. She said," They are just a toy. The firefighters don't need any more toys." Now comes the phone call.

The police officer happened to call on my shift. He said there is a gentleman that wants to meet with you. He said that this gentleman was a great friend to the police department, and that he wants to see if he can help us. The officer brought him by that evening.

Not really knowing what to expect, we were cleaning up after dinner when they stopped by. The officer introduced us to Vince. Right away, he put us at ease. He was very warm and personable. We gave him the SO-cent tour. We had a lot of pictures of fires and rescues on the walls. Vince asked questions about some of the pictures, but with almost a "kids" fascination. We sat down with coffee, and he asked why we had 3 refrigerators. We explained about the three-shift system, each one having their own place to keep leftovers, etc. So, enough of the small talk, he cut to the chase. He said, "Tell me what the city said about these cameras." I told him they said it was a toy. I explained that the Captain that I relieved this morning was the one that had done all the research and had made the proposal. Vince said that he would like to buy 2 of the cameras, one for Station 8, since that was where it originated, and one for Station 21, close to his home. I told him that the offer was incredibly generous but advised him that the cameras were $25,000 each. He just said, "Okay. Who do I make this check out to?" All I could say was someone way above my paygrade! (Spencer would have been so proud!) I called my boss, Tim, the Battalion Chief over Battalion 2. Tim asked if I thought he was serious, and when I said yes, he told me to get his contact info. Vince gave me his business card and got up to leave. On our way out, he noticed our stove with a large grill top. I explained that we were on duty for 24 hours, so we bought groceries and fixed our meals there. Vince asked if it would be possible for him to cook for us on our next shift. Of course! We all agreed. He told us to get potatoes for baked potatoes, and the ingredients for a salad. He was bringing everything else.

Vince arrived on our next shift day at 4:30. He brought 1" thick rib eyes wrapped in butcher paper. He cooked for us, and laughed so much at our picking on each other, both during and after the meal. Vince was a smoker, so I sat outside with him after dinner. We talked, we laughed, and we got to know each other. I would venture to say that over 90% of the shifts that I worked at 8's, 21's, and 10's, Vince cooked for us, or came by for lunch or coffee. We could sit and watch a baseball game, and not say a whole lot to each other. There were never any periods of uncomfortable silence. We just enjoyed each other's company. I have no idea why he treated me so well. I mentioned before that I believe God sends people in your life when they are needed. I know I received the biggest blessing from having him in my life.

Vince paid $50,000 for those first two cameras. He was the most generous person I ever met. He always wanted to remain anonymous. If he heard of a need, he met that need. A lady that had been living on the street was seen by Vince one day. He asked the same police officer to help him see what she needed. He got her an apartment and arranged caretakers for her. losing her husband had devastated her to the point of being unable to function on her own. She was homeless when Vince saw her. Two firefighters that I know developed cancer.

Vince had them sent to New York for treatment and put them and their wives in an apartment he had there. Another lost his home to a fire during construction. Vince helped him financially long before the insurance paid a dime. A man with some mental issues rode his bicycle to fire stations and fire scenes all over town. He was an easy target for thieves. When they took his bike, Vince replaced it with an even better one. I could write 1000 pages and never begin to scratch the surface about the man he was, and the impact he made on so many lives. I also could never explain why he loved us so much. I can promise you two things; none of us will EVER forget him, and we loved him right back!

Vince and his wife took Becky and I on several trips. We went on an Alaskan cruise, and on a Panama Canal cruise. On our last trip, Vince wasn't feeling well. At each port, he stayed on the ship. At the last port, he asked if I would walk with him. We got off the ship and started down the pier. About 100 yards down the pier, he stopped and told me he couldn't make it. Becky took a picture of us walking back to the boat. looking at it now, it was like an omen.

When the trip was over and we were back home, Vince called me. He said he had some bad news. "I have lung cancer." I couldn't speak for a moment. I told him that I'm so sorry to hear this. Typical Vince, he responded, "Oh well, what are you gonna do?" He invited us over for dinner that evening. Except for the nasal cannula and the oxygen concentrator, you would never know anything was different. He told us it was terminal, and already advanced. Not as a complaint, more just letting us know. I never heard him complain, even when you could tell the pain was worse. He kept a smile on his face through it all.

When our wives went to the kitchen, he called me over to his chair. He asked if I would be a pallbearer at his funeral. "It would be my honor." He said that he had not asked anyone else yet. I told him don't worry, if I have to, I will carry you myself. He let go one of his incredibly distinctive laughs.

We set up a schedule of volunteers to sit with Vince. There was never a shortage of people wanting to help. Vince had done so much for so many, and now everyone wanted to show him their love and appreciation. Vince's story with the firefighters had started that first visit at Station 8. Station 8 now had a new ladder truck, and the crew there designed a logo with a big "V" on it. The truck was named "Big V' in his honor. We had a gathering at his house and the truck pulled up to his sidewalk. We took him outside to see "Big V." The look on his face said it all! We could never repay him for all his generosity. You could never out give him. But on that evening, when he saw that truck, and knew what it meant, I think he could tell the impact he had on all our lives, and how much we loved him.

You never want to admit it, but he was growing weaker each visit. The time came when his doctor advised his family to move him to a hospice facility. That did not mean the vigil was over, it just changed location. I stopped by one morning to sit with him. When I got to his room, they told me he was getting a bath. An orderly came to the room and said he needed help getting him out of the tub. Vince had sent the orderly to get me. As I went down the hall, I could hear Vince's laugh.

The orderly was a small, young guy. Vince wasn't a large man, but he was all wet. I had Vince put his arms around my neck. I slipped my arm behind his knees and picked him up. Before I sat him in his wheelchair, he squeezed my neck, kissed my cheek, and said "I love you." I sat him in his chair, kissed his cheek, and told him I loved him, too. He never would have had to say it, I already knew. I hope he knew as well.

A few days later, a small group of us had met at the hospice. His wife and both daughters were with him. His daughter Karol came out desperately scanning the faces in the crowd. She came up to me and asked if I could stay with him that night and watch over him. Karol said they were all exhausted, and they were afraid he may need something during the night, and they wouldn't hear him. I sat in a chair at the end of his bed. His wife and daughters laid down and were quickly asleep. The nurse came in and told me to push the button on his pain meds if he started moaning. She said you can't over medicate him. The machine won't allow it. I spent the night in that chair while they slept. I thought of all the people's lives he had touched. I thought about watching baseball games with him, and about seeing him drive up at 4:30 to cook for us. I thought about how much I was going to miss him. I severely underestimated.

When he awoke the next morning, you could see the pain etched on his face, but he never complained. His breathing became difficult, and the hospice nurse came in. Vince's wife asked us all to tell him everything would be okay. Tell him you love him and will see him again in Heaven. For one split second I was back in the ICU with my dad. Tears burned my cheeks. I told him that I loved him, and that I would see him again. I thanked him for everything. His breathing slowed, and then it stopped. I called Becky and told her that he was gone. I called the station and asked them to let everyone know. I left the hospice and just drove around. I felt physically ill. I pulled into a parking lot and thanked God for putting Vince in my life. There will never be another like him.

Every time I watch a baseball game or hear a distinctive laugh, I can see his face. He's still smiling.

With all the contributions Vince had made to the fire service, our Fire Chief made him an Honorary Firefighter. He was given a full fire department funeral. The Honor Guard stood watch from the funeral home until the service began.

Bagpipes playing "Amazing Grace" in one of the largest churches in Fort Worth. An ocean of blue uniforms, police officers, friends from Vince's baseball days, and countless others were all there to pay their respect to him. The former mayor of Fort Worth, Mike Moncrief spoke at the service. Mayor Mike was also a regular visitor at Station 8. Mike and his beautiful wife Rosie had visited Vince at home, and at the hospice.

A few days before the service, Mayor Mike stopped by. He asked if we had any stories about Vince that were lighthearted, or even funny. I told him two things that came to mind: Anytime that Vince was at the station, unless was right in the middle of cooking, he responded on the truck with us. One night, he went to a fire with us that took a little while to put out. Vince needed to pee. We told him just go behind the house and pee there. He said, "No way!" Vince had seen our fire department photographer on the scene, and he didn't want to be pictured in the paper, "Vince puts the finishing touch on this house fire!"

Another time, Vince sat outside Station 8 to smoke. The ashtray he was using was a tall, metal container. Vince had not noticed that the bottom of the container was full of dry leaves. When Vince tossed his cigarette in the can, it must have ignited the leaves. The kitchen crew was preparing dinner when they noticed smoke coming from the patio. Vince was so embarrassed. One of the crew from Station 8 worked an overtime day at Station 10 and told us the story. When Vince came to cook dinner that evening, he went outside to smoke. The firefighter said, "Just a minute." The firefighter put on his bunker coat, grabbed an extinguisher, and came back outside. Then he told Vince, "Okay, light it up!" I can still hear Vince laughing.

As usual, Vince was the epitome of a host. Even at his own funeral. All of us were invited to have dinner after the service in a beautiful venue in downtown Fort Worth. He had made all these arrangements before he passed away.

Last days

Before Vince had gotten sick, I had been promoted to Battalion Chief. I ended up, before I retired, at Station 10, back on the south side of Fort Worth. As part of the promotion, they hold a "Badge Pinning" ceremony. You remove the badge from the previous rank and have the person of your choosing pin on your new one. I asked Vince to pin on my badge, and he honored me by doing so. He was one of a kind. He was generous to a fault, as kindhearted as anyone I've ever met, and loved us all FIERCELY! He freely gave, never expecting or accepting repayment. He was the greatest person I've ever known. I will miss him as long as I live. RIP Vince.

The police officer that brought Vince to our station that first night told me this story about meeting Vince: The police department wanted to outfit all of their officers with bulletproof vests. The City Manager said that would be too costly, so they would purchase some each year until everyone had one. Vince was on a plane getting ready to go to Las Vegas. He read the article, got off the plane, got on the phone and donated all the funds needed to cover the shortage. That's the Vince I know.

Cancer

Late in my career, I learned that I had prostate cancer. My dad and all his siblings had passed away in their 50's, so I thought it was just my time. I have been around death and dying for long enough to understand that it's inevitable. Life is terminal. I accepted what I thought was my fate, but then I noticed how Becky wasn't handling this chapter so well. I couldn't stand seeing her so sad all the time, so I changed my outlook.

I began researching what worked for others, and even what didn't. The one constant in all that I read was the need to remain "positive." Up until the diagnosis, I had always been a positive person. Why would I change now?

My new approach was to fight. With every fiber of my being. I recovered very quickly after the surgery. I never needed chemo or radiation. Once again, God watched over my healing. He answered our prayers. Again. As of this writing I'm 12 years cancer free. I can't believe I was ready to call it quits. I would have missed so much. I had actually started writing parts of this years ago. I put it away when I realized I was sick. Once I retired, I cleaned out my locker, and threw my start on this book away. It's been on my mind for years. I know that eventually God will call me home. Until that day, I will live each day with gratitude. I believe you can wake up hateful or grateful. It's your choice. I also believe the saying, "What you focus on expands." If you focus on bad or ugly things, they are all you see. But, if you focus on good or beautiful things, they are around you in abundance. I'm not talking about looking at life through rose colored glasses. I'm talking about beautiful sunrises or sunsets, the smiling face of a child, the love of a pet. Try it for 1 week. Look for everything good and beautiful. It will change your life!

You could tell what was going to happen. You could also tell how it was going to end. For years, almost every day, my dad would come home after working all day. When his car pulled in the driveway, he would come in through the side door.

There was never a hug, kiss or even asking about how his day went. It was always something negative, with the intention of starting a fight.

My dad was a big guy. About 6 foot tall, and around 22Slbs. He had a barrel chest, with big arms and shoulders. He was a blue-collar worker. Everything physical. In contrast, my mom was small. Probably 5'1" and around 100Ibs. Picture Foghorn Leghorn and the Chickenhawk, except there wasn't anything funny about this.

I know my dad was tired when he got home. You could see it in his face and his body language. Maybe he just knew what he was walking into. I told you before, my mom had no filter. If it was in her mind, it came out of her mouth. The first words out of her mouth would light the fuse.

Apparently, my lack of patience was not inherited from my dad. No matter how many times she tried to get a reaction out of him, he just walked into the house.

Dinnertime was usually quiet. Like the calm before the storm. If the negative comments started up again after dinner, it was going to be a long night.

I don't remember any of these problems before we moved to Fort Worth. Maybe I was too young to understand. I also don't remember any displays of affection or anything expressing appreciation. Even just writing this makes me feel sorry for him. I'm glad he didn't just drive off one day and try to find happiness. I'm not sure I could have stuck it out if he did.

After dinner, my dad would move to the couch. If my mom was in full tilt now, she wouldn't let him relax or unwind. If I could take her negative comments, her belittling venom, it's because I learned it from him. If she felt that he was not taking her seriously, or worse, ignoring her, she would explode! She would slap his face, Hard. If there was still no response, she would start rapidly slapping his face with both hands. When he raised his arms to protect his face, she would start kicking him. The next heard was a deep, tense voice saying, "That's enough." I do remember a few times that she did stop, at least momentarily. It was like a truce had been called. Most of the time it was just a pause. The look on my dad's face, the way his jaw was set, would have made grown men step back. I know she had to notice and remember how this had turned out every time she did these things.

Rising from the couch, he would step toward the side door. Then her barrage of slaps and kicks would intensify. I'm not an advocate of a man ever striking a woman. I'm also not an advocate of a woman striking a man, unless he is trying to physically assault her. You can see where this is heading.

My dad would grab her wrists and push her. She always fell, but sometimes I felt it was for a dramatic effect. On a couple of occasions, she would land a hard slap on his face. A very short, quick backhand would send her sprawling across the room. Then came the sobbing waterworks.

My big sister and I sat in the corner, side by side, with my little brother behind us. One night, as soon as the fight started, I put the neck of my t-shirt in my mouth, grinding my teeth on it, until I made a hole. When my mom hit the floor and began sobbing, I crawled over to her and asked, "WHY don't you just shut up? You know what's going to happen."

Around this same time, I developed a stutter. Mine was the kind where I could get maybe a syllable or two out, and then get hung up with what's next. I sounded like someone trying to start a car with a weak battery. I never went to speech therapy, or even saw a doctor, but to my mind, it was stress related. It lasted for several years. I think that's a big reason that I don't like public speaking. Whenever I speak, I get nervous. When I get nervous, I fumble over my words and get frustrated.

The next morning after my dad left for work, my mom came into my room. She threw back my covers and pulled me over onto my stomach. She started hitting the back of my legs and my butt with a round metal curtain rod. Through clenched teeth, she told me not to ever tell her to shut up again. The words came out more like a hiss. The rod left red welts from my lower back down to the back of my knees. As my sister and I were leaving for school, my mom pulled me back inside and warned me not to tell anyone what she had done. I was supposed to say I fell off my bike. She said if I told what she had done, it would be 10 times worse the next chance she got. I had no reason not to believe her.

A few days later, the welts were dark bruises. My sister saw them and asked what happened. My mom overheard the question, walked over to us and slapped Brenda. My sister turned away, balled up her fist, and spun back around. She punched my mom in the gut, so hard. My mom went to her knees. Brenda spoke in my mom's ear and said, "Don't you ever touch me again. If you do, I will tell my daddy what you did to him!" One look at my sister's face convinced my mom that Brenda was serious. I believe my mom knew what would happen to her if my dad found out. Brenda was my new hero!

I never saw my mom administer any punishment to Brenda after that day. My mom would tell my dad things to get Brenda in trouble, but never when Brenda was within earshot. I'm not going to lie, that episode with my mom, made I difficult for me to have any sympathy for her. I lost the respect I had for her and put the first brick in the wall between us.

After a little time had passed, I thought maybe I wasn't trying hard enough to be a "good" kid. Keep quiet, pay attention in school and in church, keep getting good grades, and so on. No matter what I tried, nothing was working. I took a long time for me to understand. It wasn't me. My mom was redirecting her anger at my dad, about everything that made her unhappy, to me. She had to have an outlet for all the pent-up hate, the meanness, whatever. Each time I would change my behavior to attempt to please her, it would not work. Always striking me when no one was around, and later, acting like nothing happened. She made my life a living hell until my dad died. A lot of hope I had of her behavior being brought to light, died with him. Now, there were no more threats of anyone telling him. It had to stop.

I know I already mentioned that I missed a lot of school after my dad passed away. I worked. A lot. For a while, there was no sense of direction for me. I just felt lost. Brenda was married, and they had moved from the neighborhood. I visited them when I had a chance. I don't really know if I worked so much because we needed the money, or because I couldn't stand being around my mom. Every day became more contentious. Everything came to a head one Friday night.

I took a girl I liked to a high school football game. I had asked for the night off from work to be able to go. I had a great time. Until I got home. My mom came into my room as I was getting ready for bed. She asked what I thought I was doing missing work to go watch a game. I told her that I was getting ready for bed, and to leave me alone. She drew back her hand to slap me, but I caught her wrist. She tried to pull free, and I pushed her out of my room. I don't know what I would have done if she had hit me. I may have changed my own beliefs about not hitting a woman. I'm glad I didn't have to find out. After that night, she never even tried to hit me again. A small victory, but more bricks were being added to the wall I was building between us.

I guess the moral to this part of my story is this; If you continue to mistreat people in your life, they will avoid you, and maybe never forgive you. When that happens, you have both lost. I'm working on the forgiveness part. If I had been a bad kid, or always given her grief, maybe I could understand, maybe even justify her actions toward me.

I moved out of my mom's house 3 weeks after my 18th birthday. I went to the courthouse and got married. I very seldom went back. I cried at my mom's funeral, not for how I felt about her, but for what could have been.

I believe there are varying levels and forms of abuse. Everybody thinks about physical or sexual abuse. Sometimes it's a combination of forms. I know lots of people had it much worse than I did. That doesn't make forgiveness any easier. Everyone that is on the receiving end of any type of abuse carries scars that may never be seen. Some keep the cycle of abuse alive with their own family.

My cousin Mary, and my wife Becky, are the only family members that know I'm writing this story. Though they may not agree with some of the things I've said about my mom, we've shared some of these thoughts when we've spent time together. Mary used to spend part of the summer with us, so she may have witnessed some of the mood swings from my mom. Becky witnessed firsthand some of the hateful things that spewed from my mom's mouth. My aunt Rosemary, Mary's mom, avoided even speaking with my mom late in life for that same reason. Rosemary and my mom were close in age and lived close to each other for years. If any of the people in her life avoiding her bothered my mom, she never seemed to care. If anything, it seemed to be more vocal about things she said.

I need to close this part on a positive note. Some of the most hateful things and hurtful things my mom said, or did to me, helped make me what I am today. I turned the negatives into motivation. If she said that I couldn't do something, that just drove me to prove her wrong. I don't know why she said some of the things she did, but I promised myself a long time ago, that I would never knowingly say anything that might hurt someone's feelings. So many of the bad things that happened were because she didn't have a filter. I will gladly blame it on her upbringing as a kid in rural Arkansas, but none of her family that I've ever met shared her same disposition. Maybe she was just unhappy. If that was the case, I would feel sorry for her. I hope she had at least some happy moments in her childhood, some good memories.

Her mother passed away before I was born. She died in a fire. My mom and dad found her. She never spoke about it, so I'm not sure how it affected her. I can't even imagine. Her dad died when I was 5 or 6. She never seemed to be close with anyone. Like my brother, she didn't seem to have any close friends. That alone has made my life so incredible. Between childhood friends like Jeff, and my brothers and sisters on the Fire department, and my wonderful friends in my neighborhood, I'm blessed beyond measure! I cherish them all!

One memory I have that's funny now but wasn't at the time; I had been saving my paper route money for a Kmart weight set. I hid the money under my mattress for a couple of months. I knew exactly how much I needed, and when I had the last portion to add, I went to retrieve my stash. It was GONE! All of it. My mom found it when she changed my sheets. She had taken it to a hair salon and had her hair done. I was so mad! I still got the weight set a few months later, and she started helping me with my paper route, especially on Sundays when the papers were so big. I guess she was trying to repay me, or she just felt guilty.

I haven't told you any of this to get your pity. To me, pity and jealousy are wasted emotions. I know a lot of people had it much worse. But I also know what could have been. Families like Jeff's surrounded him with love and support. His stepdad adopted him early on. He doted over Jeff like he was his own flesh and blood.

I really have no idea why my mom acted the way she did. I do know that I chose not to be that way. Sometimes I think I have too much of a filter. I try my best not to hurt anyone's feelings with something I say. I speak calmly and softly most of the time. I have even become more patient as I grow older. It's about time! The temper I inherited from both sides has remained mostly in check since I met Becky. I think she may disagree a little and would probably relate a story of our first date. That story won't be included here. I'm better now than I was then.

If any of the things I've written about my mom give the impression that I hated her, that's not true. I didn't understand what made her so angry, especially with my dad. I don't know what all the hateful things she would say sounded like to her when she said them. Surely she could see the hurt on people's faces. And I will never understand why I became the surrogate punching bag when she quit attacking my dad. I don't know why he stayed, but I'm so glad he did.

My Dad

The tattoo on his forearm was my favorite. It ran from his wrist to his elbow, on the inside of his arm. I believe he got it while in the Navy. The artwork and detail were incredible. It was a serpent wrapped around a dagger. Any time he turned his hand, the serpent seemed to constrict the knife. When his forearm relaxed, so did the snake. It was very hypnotic to me.

He loved to watch me play baseball. When I pitched, he sat on the center portion of the bleachers. I could see his head just above the umpire's. I had nailed a piece of paneling to our garage wall in the backyard. I had a small, round target for the strike zone, and a hard rubber baseball. I threw almost every day. You would think the constant thudding of the ball would drive him crazy, but he never complained.

My dad worked on people's cars for extra money. He also welded metal racks for trash cans and cut and welded barbecue pits out of barrels. I know he liked building things and working with his hands. I also think it was his way of avoiding some of the confrontations inside the house.

My parents met a family on the next block. My mom and this other "no filter" lady seemed to get along. My dad didn't care for her but enjoyed the husband's company. One day, my dad went to help them unload a console color TV. They carried it inside, and my dad sat down to watch it. Our TV was black and white at that time. Something in the wall between the kitchen and the garage caught fire. The small house started filling with smoke. My dad picked up their 2 young kids, one under each arm and carried them outside. His friend was still inside. My dad ran back to the door and called his name. Smoke was coming out the front doorway. My dad found his friend trying to carry out the new TV. His friend never even asked about his kids. A lot of things people do require a license; drive a car, open a business, or get married. But anybody can have kids. No training, no requirements. Maybe some people should not have kids. My mom would fit that category. My opinion.

After the fire, my dad seemed to spend less time with his friend. I think he saw a different side of him that day, and that it bothered him. Those neighbors moved away, and we went to their new place a couple of times. The relationship had changed, and they just drifted apart.

One night I was collecting money for my paper route. It was dark, but I was on my next to the last street. As I walked down the street, 2 guys stepped out from behind a van and pushed me up against it. I had most of my money in a zippered bank bag. I still had a $10 dollar bill in my hand from my last customer. One of them grabbed the money in my hand, and the other one put the tip of a knife under my chin. The one with the knife grabbed the bank bag, but I wouldn't let go. Most of the money in the bag was to pay for the papers. Only a portion was mine. I knew we didn't have extra money to pay for anything I lost, so I held on tight. The knife was pushed into the soft skin, making a little cut under my chin. A neighbor heard his dog barking and came out to investigate.

He was holding a shotgun and a flashlight. Both boys took off running. I hurried home. My dad walked by my room and saw me holding a Kleenex on my chin. I told him what happened. I never expected to see them again. The next night they were in my yard. They said they needed more money. I said I would have to go inside to get some. Not the brightest thieves! I went inside and told my dad they were outside. He went outside with a hunting rifle. He gave them a look that was chilling. He told them to leave and never come back. For just a moment, I felt sorry for them.

I saw one of them a few days later at my school. He turned away from me and hurried down the halt. I saw him one other time. He told me the guy with the knife was his cousin. The cousin had been arrested and was in serious trouble. He told me he realty thought my dad was going to shoot them. I remember thinking the same thing. Maybe this guy had a really bad upbringing. He learned the hard way that all actions and decisions have consequences. That's got to be one of the worst things to learn the hard way.

I don't believe my dad was ever happy at his job at the box factory. He did alt the maintenance on the forklifts and conveyors, but it was indoors and mundane. The first time I went with him to start building a house, you could see the joy and excitement on his face. He started building custom homes at a great time.

Business was good, and he developed a great reputation. Later on, business slowed down, and he decided to take the written test in order to join the Carpenter's Local Union. Now remember, I told you he dropped out of school. My mom was so worried that he would fail the test. I felt bad that she didn't offer him any encouragement or support. He was gone a long time that day. I know he was probably nervous, but I believe he had confidence in his abilities.

He came in that day with one of the biggest smiles! He was now a Journeyman Carpenter. The construction business, especially new home construction, took a big downturn. Even the Union jobs were rare. For a while my dad was able to get by doing remodel jobs. I didn't help as often with these, but the stress he felt to provide for his family was apparent to all of us.

I remember the look on his face the first time he asked if I had any paper route money. He was looking for work and needed gas for his truck. He couldn't look me in the eye. I was happy to be able to help. I gave him all I had, probably less than $20. I know it hurt him to ask, and I will never forget the look on his face.

The frequency of these requests became more numerous. The look on his face became more depressed and was now joined with a look of shame. We had been through some tough times before, but not this long. Or this tough.

I think in our neighborhood, most were aware of the financial difficulties my family was facing. It seems like most of my route customers also bought seeds from me. One lady asked if I had tried other neighborhoods. So, this shy little kid ventured out to try and make some money.

The first house I tried out of my comfort zone, was a very nice lady. She not only ordered seeds, she told me about a way to sell personalized Christmas cards!

Seeds in the Spring and Fall, Christmas cards in the Winter. I even picked up a few new customers on my paper route! Talk about answered prayers!

I know that even in those days an extra $20 to $30 dollars wouldn't pay the bills. It would buy enough food for a few days, but that's about all. I did really well with selling both the seeds and the Christmas cards. My dad had a few people that owed him money for work he had done.

Soon, they wouldn't answer the phone or knock on the door. Eventually things started to improve, and we were able to get caught up on most things. A man called and asked my dad to build a house for him from a "kit", in Tyler.

The first day, we left early and worked all day. Driving back that evening, my dad realized this commute wasn't practical. I knew he needed and wanted to work, so we packed the truck for a week, and camped out in Tyler every night. It was the most one-on-one time I ever got to spend with my dad. He still didn't talk a lot, but he did something I really needed. He listened.

I felt more comfortable around him now. Being with him away from home was a real treat. I hope he enjoyed it as much as I did. He was working, which improved his mood, and he was having fun camping. We camped out some when I was growing up. This campground had a nice sized lake, and we got to fish. He spent some time showing me how to tie on a lure and rested his arm on my shoulder as I tried to do it myself. My only remembrance of his touch.

Whenever we were lucky enough to catch some fish, he would clean them and cook them for our dinner. I know now that I was the lucky one. None of my siblings ever had that one-on-one time with him. They never got to see him this happy, this relaxed. His mood improved so much he even started to tease and kid around with me. I had grown accustomed to hearing him talk. Now I got to hear him laugh.

A few times I caught myself wanting to tell him about how my mom treated me when he was at work. Fear for her safety was the only thing that kept me from doing so. I was truly afraid he would kill her. Then I would lose them both.

By the end of the summer, we were through with the kit house. As small as I was, I could now put a bundle of shingles on my shoulder and climb the ladder with them. One day, on a hot ride home, I almost caused WWIII.

My dad would stop at a store on our way home. He would reach into a large tub by the register and grab a beer. He would tell me to get a coke, and he would usually get a hot link sandwich. Something about seeing the sweat running down that cold beer can made my mouth water. He saw the look on my face and asked if I wanted to try one. He warned me and said if I did, I could NEVER tell my mom! I promised.

You've no doubt seen the dogs that can sniff out drugs if you walk them by the luggage. My mom could sniff out beer before you pulled in the driveway. My dad told me "Don't go near your mom!" Like some rite-of-passage, I just wanted to have my first beer with my dad. My dad just wanted us to survive the minefield that awaited us! My dad said that I would have to acquire a taste for beer. I took my first sip and knew I was in trouble...! Loved It! I took bigger sips, gradually swallowing mouthfuls. After drinking around¾ of the beer, I was getting full. I weighed less than 80lbs, and I had not eaten much for lunch. And I drank this part fast! So, full and a little buzzed. We pulled in the driveway, and my mom stepped out of the side door, on full alert. My dad intercepted her and kept himself between us. I hustled into the house and went to my room. A few minutes later, my dad came in and told me to lay down. He had told my mom that I got overheated out in the sun today. I know he took a big chance by letting me try the beer. I would give everything I own to have one more beer with him right now.

One more bragging story about my dad. During a remodel, we were removing a wall to open up a room. We had braced the ceiling up with 2x4s until we could span that gap with a steel beam. The beam weighed close to 500 lbs. My dad was on one end, and my brother-in-law, the homeowner, and I took the other. We had to climb up and put it in place. My dad held his end while we wrestled our end all around and finally placed it correctly. The homeowner commented on my dad having to hold his end by himself the entire time, climb up unassisted, and place the beam. I had witnessed him lifting things before that I knew were very heavy, so I knew he was strong. This was a different kind of strong. I can't tell you how impressed I was, and how proud. Later in my life, God blessed me with more strength that I ever dreamed possible. I still could not have held a candle to my dad.

Thank you, God, for the one-on-one time I got to spend with my dad.

I believe my dad would have been proud of my work as a firefighter. I know that he would have been proud of how hard I worked to get there. My mom was negative after my first failed test. That all changed when I finally made it. She would tell complete strangers that her son was a firefighter.

In her last years, she became acquainted with all the firefighters from Station 30. She called them all the time. When she fell and broke her hip, they came to her rescue. During panic attacks and when she exhibited the first signs of dementia, the firefighters were her guardian angels. My first observation of her mental health issues was when she couldn't remember the names of the responders.

Some members of Station 30's crew called me, concerned about her wellbeing. At most of the stations where I worked, there always seemed to be at least one person that regularly called for help. Some of these were probably just lonely, some had obvious mental health issues, and no one to help them. There were even a few that were unable to do things by themselves. We changed smoke detector batteries and changed out water bottles on the big dispensers. Falls were very common reasons for calling. If the situation was mental health related or chronic medical issues, there are agencies we could contact for help. Then, there are the people that believed that if you went to the hospital by ambulance, you would move to the front of the line. Unfortunately for them, the more severe injuries and illnesses are first priority. The walk-ins, and the ambulance transports are all sorted by the gatekeepers. The last category, in my opinion, abuses the system. They are the "frequent flyers" that call 9-1-1as a taxi service. I believe toward the end of her life, my mom fit this category.

With the number of medical rising each year, it's no wonder that firefighters are experiencing burn-out from the workload. Divorce rates are high among first responders. Sleep cycles are another concern. Thankfully, there are programs available to these responders. The most helpful to me personally were the "Critical Incident Stress Management" teams. If the Incident Commander felt the situation warranted it, a CISM team could be requested. The death or severe injuries to children, catastrophic injuries, or multiple casualties are examples of calls that might call for a "debriefing."

I mentioned before about the crew returning to the station after a bad call and starting to talk about it as a group. The problem I see with this lies in the fact that all people handle this type of stress differently. Firefighters with young children may react more emotionally than a single person. Another problem arises when the firefighter{s) keep all their emotions in check, hiding all the parts that really bother them. The debriefings I attended at least presented an opportunity to vent those feelings in a safe environment.

The members of these CISM teams are all volunteers. They normally receive formal training and are definitely life savers. All comments from a debriefing are confidential, and members are chosen with that understanding. I've never learned how these teams vent their own emotions after a debriefing, but there must be an outlet for this. I don't recommend telling your spouse about a bad incident. You telling them may help you feel better, but what does it do to them? The same would seem to apply to the debriefing team. They are usually only used on the worst calls. How do these members vent, and to whom? I've wondered if individuals such as pediatric doctors and nurses have a similar relief system in place.

A good Incident Commander watches their crews closely for anything that could cause them harm. Mental health of the responders could be at risk of injury with these type calls. Take care of your people. And yourself.

Salvation

One morning on our drive to work, I was sitting between my brother-in-law, David Sr., and my dad. I don't remember how the subject came up, but they were discussing belief in God. My mom drug us to church every time the doors were open. My dad and my sister Brenda rarely attended. For my dad, very rarely.

David Sr. asked my dad, "Do you believe in God?" Without pause, my dad answered, "Yes, I believe." Being there to witness that conversation gave me comfort when he died. It bothered me a little at first. I thought about his unwillingness to go to church with us, and wondered if he should have been baptized. Then I remembered the story of the thief on the cross. Jesus was crucified between two thieves. One of them refused to believe. The other one said, "Lord, remember me when you come into your Kingdom." That thief was never baptized. Jesus accepts his repentance and gives him the promise that the thief will be with him in paradise. I took great comfort in this scripture.

The preacher from our little Baptist church came by a few days before the funeral. He asked if my dad was saved. My mom started to cry and said she really didn't know. I told them about the conversation from years ago. I looked at my mom's face; saw she was still crying. The preacher asked if he was ever baptized. When I said I don't know, my mom cried even harder. I asked the preacher about the thief on the cross. The thief had never been baptized. Jesus accepted the thief's repentance and promised him eternal life. No baptism, no church attendance, just a belief.

Before my mom passed, she talked about my dad being in the room with her. I don't know if he was there, but it gave her peace and comfort when she saw him. I've attended enough funerals to understand that the message needs to give the family at least a glimmer of hope. A hope that they will spend eternity together in Heaven. I take comfort in knowing that my dad believed.

John 11:26 'Truly, truly, I tell you, he who believes has eternal life."

Maggie and Snoop

There are two small cloth bags in my closet. They hold the ashes from the two dogs that taught me so much about unconditional love. I wouldn't feel right if I didn't feel right if I didn't share how much they meant to me. To us.

Maggie was the first "indoor" dog I ever had. Becky and I were empty nesters for the first time since we married. Becky really wanted a dog. She begged me to let her get one, but I held firm. Well, kinda.

One of Becky's coworkers knew of a neighbor with a litter of blonde lab pups. I made the mistake of agreeing to go see them. I think Maggie was the last female left. The neighborhood kids called her "Lucy" and took turns carrying her around. Her little paws rarely touched the ground. One look at that little ball of fur, and I knew she was going home with us.

So, if you take into account that she came pre-spoiled, and you add in the love that Becky had for her from first sight, and I knew life would never be the same. I just didn't know it would be so much better.

The First Night

Maggie had been around her siblings, around her mother, and loved on and carried around every day. Becky had spent all evening playing with her and loving on her. She made Maggie a nice bed next to ours and laid her down to sleep. The saddest little whimpers started at a low volume. Soon, as the night wore on, they became louder and longer. Becky's attempts to console her were short lived at best. Maggie was really pouring on the "poor, pitiful me," cries. Becky is the soft hearted one and she couldn't take it anymore. Becky lay on the floor next to Maggie that first night, and several more in the beginning. Silly me, I thought now Becky would see that dogs belong outside. Maggie was about to teach me lesson #1...dogs are special!

When Maggie went in to be spayed, she came out wearing the famous "cone." She was still pretty well out of it from the procedure. She just laid around for a while. As she started to come around, I began to feel sorry for her. She looked so uncomfortable! Those big, brown eyes framed by the white cone, were just too much. I used the excuse that Becky needed to get some sleep, so let me sleep on the floor with her tonight. So I did. And I fell in love! Even though she had already chosen Becky as her person, she lay next to me that night and slept.

It was like sleeping next to a newborn baby. You wake to every little whimper, and you constantly check to make sure they are breathing. Okay, so maybe some dogs can stay indoors.

Maggie was very smart and was quickly housebroken. Becky took her everywhere! Maggie would get in the car and curl up in the passenger seat. They would always be together. Maggie definitely filled the void left behind when the kids moved out. We had a sunroom with a "doggy door" that went out to the back patio, and large backyard. Eventually, the time came for Becky to go back to work. Maggie couldn't understand why she had to say behind. Maggie would sit by the gate next to the garage and hang her head. She would give us the most pitiful look. With her head hung low, eyes pleading with us to take her wherever we were going. Or stay here with me and play! She would turn it on every day until we couldn't take it anymore.

Doggy Daycare

Once we found the right place, we looked at the possibility of taking her "a couple of days each week" to the same location as our vet at the time. Those "couple of days" quickly turned into most days, and she loved it! Ask her in the morning, "Want to go to school?" and she would beat you to the car. Once we got there, she could pull you to the door, and then drag you to the back. By now, she was bigger, but she loved being in with the smaller dogs. She was so gentle with them. Looking back, she would have been a wonderful mom.

All the workers loved her and greeted her by name when she came in. While it filled the void, she felt from being left alone, it became expensive. We thought maybe she could use a partner. I probably don't have to tell you this, but by now, except for Becky, Maggie was the most spoiled thing in our house!

Snoop

We were talking about getting another dog to keep Maggie company. Becky looked at a website for a shelter in Fort Worth. The shelter recommended a "meet and greet" for the dogs. Becky found one that seemed a good match. His name was "Donovan." He was a lab-chow mix. He had the lab frame, covered with chow fur. Becky took Maggie to meet him, and she was not impressed. Maggie was used to being the "Queen" and this shelter dog didn't impress her one bit!

For Snoop, (I will explain the name change) it was love at first sight! The ride home was comical. Snoop jumped right in and moved over next to Maggie. She walked to the back corner, as far away as she could get, turned her back to him, and sat down. What a little Diva!

So, about the name, Donovan. Becky and I are lifelong Dallas Cowboy fans. We couldn't bring ourselves to call our dog "Donovan" since Donovan McNabb was the Philadelphia Evils, sorry, Eagles QB for years. Becky named him Snoop and called him Snoop Dog most of the time. If anyone called him "Snoopy', she quickly corrected them.

All the ride home, Snoop tried to make friends with Maggie, when we got to our house, we took them both to the backyard. I'm not sure how long Snoop had been at the shelter, but as soon as I let him go, he was off like he had been shot out of a cannon! He ran several laps around our big backyard. After stretching his legs, he came and sat down between us. Maggie tried her best to seem unimpressed with this new guy, but I saw her watching him. When he stopped, he looked so content.

I almost felt like I was betraying my first dog, George. I found myself drawn to Snoop, and he responded by picking me as his "person". I think it would have caused a lot of dissension if Snoop had picked Becky. Maggie was a world champion pouter! But, as hard as Maggie tried to pretend that she didn't approve of our latest addition, you could tell that she loved him. She put on a front to make you believe she didn't, but you could see right through it.

Their personalities were so different, so unique. Snoop was bigger, more muscular. Maggie wasn't prissy, but she was feminine. Maggie basically educated Snoop about life in our home. She taught him to use the doggy door and had him housebroken quickly. Even though Snoop was larger, more powerful, he respected Maggie's place in the family, and did her bidding. She had him trained in no time!

After I retired, we had a house built in a beautiful subdivision. There were only about 100 homes at that time, sitting on 5000 acres of God's Beauty! I started walking them in the mornings, and it was not uncommon to be outside with them for hours without seeing another person, or even another vehicle. Some of my most enjoyable times were walking them around a loop. It was 3 miles, and took us a little while to complete, but I loved it! And so did they!

AS time turned into years, the walks got shorter. Maggie started having some difficulty with her hips. Whenever she started limping, we would turn back toward the house. Sometimes Snoop and I would go back to finish the walk, but it wasn't the same. Maggie would be waiting at the front door when we returned, looking sad that she didn't get to go, but happy that we were home.

Some mornings, Becky would go with us. She would take Maggie's leash, and I would take Snoop's. One of my favorite memories of our time with them happened on such a morning. The four of us left the house. Before we had gone very far, Maggie began to slow down. Even with the limp, she never really wanted to go back home. On this particular morning, Becky said that she would take Maggie home. She told me to go ahead and finish the walk with Snoop. As Becky and Maggie turned toward the house, Snoop and I turned to leave. Every few steps, the dogs would turn and look at each other. After just a few minutes, Maggie stopped. Snoop stopped as well.

They both pulled toward each other. We decided to drop the leashes and let them go. They ran toward each other, something I had never seen them do. When they reached each other, you would have thought we had kept them apart for weeks! Tails wagging, nose to nose, both so excited. Then, the biggest surprise for me, Maggie kissed Snoop! The little Diva dropped her mask for a moment! I would give anything to have had a picture of that! Pure love! Don't ever try to tell me that dogs don't have a soul.

I was working a part time job in Minnesota when Becky called. I could tell she had been crying. She told me that Snoop couldn't get up, and that she could tell he felt really bad. She was taking him to our vet. One of the vet techs helped her carry him inside. After the exam, she sent me his picture. He looked so sad, like he had somehow let us down. That picture was heartbreaking! The vet told Becky that Snoop was in very bad shape. I knew that she didn't want him to suffer, but she wanted me to be able to see him and hold him one more time. He was really hurting. It was time to let him go.

Becky laid on the floor, her arms wrapped around him. She told him how much we loved him, and what a good boy he was. He went peacefully with her holding him. She called me, crying so hard. I knew then he was gone. That was one of the worst days, one of the longest days, of my life.

A few days later, Maggie walked up to Becky, and laid her head in Becky's lap. Becky told me that Maggie let out the most mournful sound, something she had never heard before. She howled, moaned, and whimpered at the same time. She was crying for her friend! That was her grieving for Snoop. That was pouring out her soul for her soulmate! I don't think Maggie ever got over losing Snoop. I know I didn't.

Maggie's hip seemed to decline even more now. The playfulness was gone. She slept more now, but still wagged her tail when she saw us or heard our voice. She wanted to cuddle more. To just be held.

Becky was at work when Maggie limped over to me. Maggie laid her head on my lap, and just looked up at me. She was in pain. Now it was my turn to make a decision. I took her to the vet, praying all the way. I wanted so badly for the vet to give her something to make her feel better and let me take her home. The vet checked her out and took X-rays. The bone in one of her legs had deteriorated so badly, he wasn't sure how she could stand. I believe she knew how bad she was. I asked the vet, "IF she were your dog, what would you do?" He told me the humane thing would be to put her down. He said if that bone breaks, the cry of pain she makes will haunt you forever!

The vet and the tech left me alone with Maggie for a while. I held her in my lap, with her head on my shoulder. It felt more like she was trying to comfort me.

When the vet and tech came back, I was rocking her with tears streaming down my cheeks, just like I'm doing now. If that causes you to think of me as a sissy, I'm fine with that. I've held back tears too many times in my life.

I sat on the floor with Maggie's head in my lap. I touched her face as gently as I could. I just kept telling her how much we loved her. How much I loved her. I told her to go be with Snoop. I know he was waiting for her. She looked at me one last time and weakly wagged her tail. Goodbye, sweet Maggie! Thank you for teaching me about unconditional love!

I believe that when Maggie crossed over the Rainbow Bridge that Snoop was waiting. His big, bushy tail wagging non-stop! I believe they ran towards each other, completely free from pain. And I believe she kissed him.

For a couple of years, the painful memories were too much to even consider another dog. I finally convinced Becky to go to a Mega Adoption in Fort Worth. Now it was my turn to beg for a dog! We walked by a bunch of pens. Dogs of all shapes and sizes. As we passed by one pen, I saw a dog sitting back in the corner. There was just something about him. We went in and spent a few minutes with him. When we passed by a little later, he was at the gate like he was watching us. We were told he was an "owner surrender." His people had dropped him off at a groomer, and never came back. So, to me he was abandoned. He was house broken and knew some commands. Someone had apparently spent some time with him. At one point, maybe even loved him. I don't believe the dogs understand why their person left them. I couldn't do that.

When we made the decision to adopt him, he pulled me all the way to our truck. When I opened the door, he jumped in. We brought him home. He is just what we needed!

On his first night with us, we had a bed for him by the foot of our bed. He walked to the room with us, came to my side, and stood on his back legs. He put his paws on my chest and laid his head between them. He stayed this way for a few seconds. He then went around to Becky and did the exact same thing! We both believed he was giving us a hug! The next night, he jumped up on the bed, squeezed between us, and has slept like that ever since.

I don't think I ever realized how much "company" a dog can be. If I'm walking with him, I talk to him all the way. If I'm at home alone, he sits by me and listens when I talk to him. Whenever I leave for a work trip, or if we go on vacation, I can't wait to get home and see him. He's just as excited to see us! It melts my heart to see him get so excited, hop around, not sure if he wants to go outside and play ball, or roll over for a belly rub!

Becky

Not only would my story be incomplete, so would my life. I told you earlier that I believe God sends people into your life for a reason. We may have needed each other, but I DEFINITELY needed her. She's, my anchor. I'm the dreamer, and she listens to whatever the latest idea or scheme that I want to follow, then she tries to reason with me. Usually when she repeats my idea back to me, I can hear the skepticism in her voice. Sometimes she smiles at me while shaking her head, other times I get the "eye roll" which is telling me NO without actually saying it. Also, besides putting up with my crazy ideas, she has banned me from ordering anything on the internet! How was I supposed to know it was a subscription and I would get billed each month? In the end, she contacted the company and cancelled the purchase, but not before threatening me with bodily harm if I went on another online shopping spree.

Before I retired and we moved to our new home, we lived in Benbrook. It was a great little neighborhood with only one drawback. Most of the people weren't "neighborly." We only knew a few people around us, but no real friends. Our next-door neighbors on one side were the friendliest. Unfortunately, they moved to a Retirement Community in Tennessee. I moved them in a rented truck. We hated to see them leave! Becky started writing in a Prayer Journal. One of her entries was her asking God to please help her meet some friends.

Once we moved to our home, she was overjoyed with the genuinely friendly people living in our community. Becky is shy by nature, but you would never know it now! She has friends all over this county! She has blossomed into a complete extrovert. She never meets a stranger. The change in her is such a blessing! Most definitely an answered prayer.

Becky was looking through some things last weekend and found that journal. She read her prayer, remembering how sad she had been, and how incredible her life is now! The tears on her face were the happy kind. I'm always okay with that kind.

I first met Becky when I drove a delivery truck for a pharmaceutical company. I walked into the small pharmacy she worked at one day, and instantly fell in love! I'm serious! Of course, she wasn't as impressed with me right away. She's beautiful! She has that smile that lights up any room. I know people looking at us together must think, "That guy must be rich!" She makes me feel like the wealthiest man in the world. She loves me now and makes sure that I know it. She appreciates me, and that is priceless! She's loving and makes people wat to spend time with her. I asked God to send me someone to love and feel loved in return.

My cup runneth over!

Whenever I write Becky a note, she always cries. When she read my first couple chapters of this book, she cried. I'm not intentionally trying to turn on the waterworks, I just want her to know how much I love her. My life before her was a trainwreck. Most of the problems were self-inflicted. Some others were aftereffects of things I routinely dealt with at work. My middle initial is "R." Some of the medics we answered with saw my name on my shirt as G.R. Lee. My nickname became "Grim

Reaper." It was funny for a while. I can function in the worst-scenes, basically on autopilot. It's the after that gets me. I wasn't as good at talking through the things that bothered me as some of my coworkers. I didn't want to be considered weak or soft. Before I met Becky, I had issues with coping. The temper and anger that always sat just under the surface kept showing up. I had issues with alcohol and my main problem, road rage.

If you met me now, you hopefully would never believe any of these things to be true. I have truly changed. Becky makes me better, A better person, a better husband, a better man. I'm human and I still make mistakes. I try every day to just be better than the day before. I don't like myself when I get mad. It makes me feel sick to my stomach.

When Becky and I first married I had horrible nightmares. She would wake up to find me in a cold sweat, violently kicking off all the covers, because I thought the bed was covered in snakes. I can't explain how soothing her voice and her touch were to me. She never became impatient with me. She would put her arm around me and tell me everything is okay. She would gently touch my chest and my face with love. I know that sometimes she must have wondered what she had gotten herself into!

I was fortunate to find someone to help me talk about the nightmares. It was such a relief. One night, after a long period without any bad dreams, I rolled over in bed and felt a sharp stinging sensation on my chest. I swept my hand across the sheet and felt something on the bed. I quickly brushed it off. Since I sat up so quickly, Becky thought I was dreaming. She asked what was wrong and I said, "Something just stung me!" She gently rubbed my back telling me it was just a bad dream. I knew that I had been stung, but she had been through this too many times. I knew she was tired, but she never got angry or impatient. I got out of bed and turned on the light. There, by my closet door was the scorpion that had nailed me! A few days later I was getting dressed for work. I had laid my clothes out the night before and when I put on my shirt, I got stung several times before I could get it off. To this day, I still shake out my clothes before putting them on!

There is no doubt in my mind that Becky could have done better than marrying me. I'm so thankful that she took a chance on me and has weathered any storm right beside me. I just pray that I pass away first so I never have to live another day without her. I thank God for her daily. I pray that above all else she feels safe and loved.

Jason

Jason was four when his sister was born. Even at a young age he was a good big brother. He went to one of his sister's first checkups including an early round of inoculations. The first needle stick caused a cry of pain and started her crying. Jason jumped out of his chair and ran across the room. He angrily asked the nurse, "What did you do to my sister?" He was protective of her then and still is today.

Years later, their mom and I had been arguing. A lot. I packed some clothes and uniforms and asked the Captain at my station if I could crash in a spare bed for a few days. I wasn't the first to ask for this type of favor, and probably not the last. A couple of days later, my wife and kids came by to visit me at the station. My daughter crawled into my lap, and my son sat next to me. They told me all about their day and asked when I was coming home. I'm sure they rehearsed their lines on the way there. I came home for my kids.

Several more years passed and several more times I moved to the station for a few days. I kept trying to convince myself that it was better for the kids if their parents stayed together. A couple of my brother firefighters convinced me that maybe it wasn't. They assured me that kids are smarter than you think. They certainly realize all the tension between mom and dad. No kind words spoken and lots of slammed doors. At the end of one of our most heated arguments, I said I wanted a divorce. I believe she was actually relieved. The only thing she said was, "You have to tell your children." I didn't think it would be a big surprise to them, but I also didn't expect it to be so hard.

So, the next day when I knew how I wanted to tell them, I took them for ice cream. I thought I had rehearsed enough to make this as painless as possible. We had always been close, so I thought it would be like any other conversation we had ever had, just more serious. They both got emotional. That broke my heart. We talked about other things for a while. I assured them they were both loved very much, and that nothing they had done had brought this about. We stayed and talked until they were both somewhat ok with this decision.

I was at the station on Christmas Eve. The doorbell rang and I went to answer. A young guy read my name on my uniform and handed me an envelope. He said he had been paid extra to serve me divorce papers on Christmas Eve. Probably for just a split second, the look on my face wasn't nice. He backed away quickly while apologizing. He yelled, "Merry Christmas" as he ran for his car.

It seemed like the process took forever. I had moved into an apartment in Benbrook to stay close to my kids. I stayed involved in their lives and talked to them as often as possible. Not too long after I left, Jason called me and told me he had moved in with some friends. I'm still close with Jason. I'm not sure what life at home was like for him after I left. I'm truly sorry for any kind of unpleasant things he went through. The biggest surprise for me was the effect all of this had on my daughter.

My daughter had always been a "daddy's girl." From the time she was old enough to walk, she would meet me at the door as soon as I got home. Her favorite place was my lap for story time. Getting ready for bed each night, the routine stayed the same. She would pick a book for "us" to read. Sitting up in my lap, head resting on my chest, I would start to read. Then she would start asking questions or telling me what the book said. Even at a young age she quickly learned the story line and could name all the characters. As she got sleepy, I could feel her relaxing. Sometimes I kept reading in a quieter voice. Other times I would just enjoy this time with her and wish it would last longer than it did. A lot of nights, I would carry her to her room with her head resting on my shoulder. Gently laying her down, I would kiss her goodnight.

On any night that she was not quite asleep, we did the "Eskimo / butterfly" kiss. If you're not familiar, putting our noses side by side, we turned our heads back and forth for the Eskimo portion. The Butterfly was opening and closing our eyelashes on each other's cheek. She was a beautiful little girl and she matured into a beautiful young lady.

When it was my time to have the kids, she always seemed happy. Adjusted. As time went by, she would occasionally get upset. I thought, or hoped, that it was just a phase she was going through. A few years later she got married, and later she had my first grandson, Greg. By the time Greg was starting school, her marriage was suffering. I answered the doorbell one day and found her standing there with Greg. They needed a place to stay. She and I hadn't been getting along so well lately, so I was ecstatic! She said it was just for a little while. I brought them into the house and got them settled in the other two bedrooms. I was so happy! I didn't care how long they stayed!

She told me she needed a job. On my next shift I heard one of my friends say his wife was looking for someone to drive a van for her group home. I got the info for my daughter and called her with the news. She got hired and it paid a very generous starting wage. It seemed like everything was falling into place. We had fixed up Greg's room to be everything a little boy would want. Life was good in our house! For a while.

My daughter got fired. My friend apologized over and over. It wasn't any fault of his. I started trying to help her look for work. Becky was checking as well. After filling out a few applications with no luck, I believe my daughter gave up. We would leave for work in the mornings with her still asleep. Greg would ride the bus to school. The bus picked him up right in front of our house. Our dog, Maggie, would watch him get on and off the bus every day. Then the bickering started.

My daughter started sleeping late every morning. She wasn't the best about picking up her room. She wasn't overly concerned about taking a shower. She basically hung out at the house all day, but seldom helped around the house. She's my daughter and I love her, but she put me in a very awkward position. On top of all of this, we paid her bills and made sure she and Greg were always fed. Becky has never been one to hide her feelings, so she would ask my daughter to please help. Soon I was husband/ dad/ referee. I felt bad for letting it go so bad for so long.

Years had passed and all the things had changed. My daughter had gotten pregnant while living with us. The father was a married man. My daughter believed that he was going to get a divorce and marry her. Becky and I met him. He's a nice young man. I sat and listened to my daughter tell him all she had planned for their future. The more she talked, the more his color started to change. He looked like he had aged 20 years in 20 minutes, and his complexion made him look deathly ill. He told her he had to leave and ran out. I couldn't blame him! I actually felt sorry for him until he asked her for a paternity test.

Becky and my daughter started to clash a little more often. I wanted them to get along or at least peacefully coexist. I think I mentioned before that my daughter was tough. Pretty much a tomboy growing up. I got home one day and my daughter meets me at the door. She tells me that I had better get control of my wife! She goes on to say that she almost punched Becky for something she said. I just laughed. Becky is tough. I don't mean tough for a girl, just tough. I told my daughter that things would not have turned out the way she wanted. I should have realized then that things were coming to a head. No one ever accused me of being smart. So, one day I get phone calls from both of them. Both gave me ultimatums. The only problem was their timing. They had picked a day that had gone very badly for me.

Beautiful Little Girl

When Becky had gotten home that day, my daughter had cleaned her room! Becky complimented her on how good it looked. My daughter said, "Thanks! My boyfriend is coming for the weekend, and I want everything to look nice." When Becky called me, she could barely talk. She had asked my daughter where her boyfriend was going to stay. My daughter said she had invited him to stay here with her. Becky said that's not going to happen. He can't stay here! Now they were both mad.

That evening, I was standing between them. Both of them were yelling. My day had been long and frustrating. I try really hard to never raise my voice. I don't like being yelled at, but I needed to get their attention. I slammed my hands down on the table. I told them I love both of them but right now I don't like either of you! Quit yelling and tell me what is going on! Becky started telling the story. When she reached the part about the boyfriend spending the weekend, I stopped her. I turned to face my daughter and said, "No way!" My daughter started reciting the "I'm an adult and I can do whatever I want, blah, blah, blah!"

I reminded her that as the homeowner and dad, those decisions were up to me. She got mad and met her boyfriend somewhere else and stayed with him. Both grandkids were dropped off by their dads after being with them for the weekend. When my daughter came in that evening, she went to her room without saying a word. Probably for the best.

My daughter and her husband came to my retirement party. That was the last time I saw her. There is now another granddaughter that I have never seen. Becky feels bad for the way this all turned out. She has reached out to my daughter several times with no response.

Some people tell me to be patient, that she will eventually come around. I shake my head like I agree with them, but I'm not so sure.

For better or worse, I've made my peace with the whole thing. My grandson Greg keeps in touch with us. He and I spent a lot of time together when they lived with us. Jason let's me know how his sister is doing. If I dwell on it too long, it makes me sad. Most days I don't even think about it. I will always love her and I miss her being a part of my life. I can't make her return those feelings.

One part of me is glad this is coming to an end. Another part feels like this is the first layer. God blessed me with the ability to remember things. The flip side of that coin is that I remember everything. Memory is great when I'm preparing for a test but not so great when I'm trying to sleep. Becky says that I have "selective" hearing, so maybe I need selective remembering. I don't usually talk about the calls that live in my mind, unless they are humorous. I don't like reliving them and I don't think you really need them in your head either. I'm going to break my own rule for one incident. For some reason, this particular call has been in the forefront of my mind for the last several weeks.

At the station, I responded to incidents in a large SUV. 99.9% of the time I was by myself. I had one of the firefighters from my station with me for a couple of hours while the truck was at training. A call was dispatched in the area covered by our truck, and the closest neighboring unit was sent. My firefighter and I responded in the SUV and we were given the rest of the information,…"a reported drowning involving a child."

Anything involving a child resulted in a maximum dose of adrenaline to your system. We rushed to the scene and were directed to the backyard. There was an above ground pool with two teenage boys in the water. They were not acting the way you would expect. No anxiety, no stress. They were standing by the ladder and talking. We asked if they had called but they shook their heads no and went back to their conversation. Looking at the pool, we noticed that you could not see the bottom. An older adult came out of the backdoor and dove in. He didn't speak English but his actions spoke volumes. It was obvious that a child was missing and was somewhere in the pool. When he surfaced, he was looking left and right. He went underwater a second time and came up with a young girl, probably 3 or 4 years old. We took the girl from him and started mouth-to-mouth resuscitation.

By the time we made it to the front yard the ambulance arrived for transport. We had started CPR and my firefighter stepped into the ambulance with the young girl in his arms, still performing compressions.

As the ambulance left the scene, I noticed the grandfather. The look on his face was pure, unadulterated heartbreak. The grandfather was the one that dove in and found her. The rest of the family and some friends or neighbors were all in the front yard trying to see what happened. The mournful sounds and the flood of tears are all you see and hear. People hugging and holding on to each other. It's such a devastating atmosphere. There is nothing you can do or say. You whisper a prayer for a miraculous outcome and wipe your own eyes.

I drove to the hospital to pick up my firefighter. The look on his face told me all I needed to know. He and the medics had worked feverishly to save this beautiful child. I'm sure that plenty of whispered prayers were sent before they got to the hospital. She was pronounced shortly after arrival. Somber hugs and handshakes went around the room. We spoke very little on the way back to the station. The grief starts as a profound sadness. I feel like I have an unbearable weight on my chest making it hard to breathe and speeding up my heart. I feel my pulse pounding in my ears. Then I think, if it's this bad for me, how much worse is it for the family?

I really should have talked with the firefighter on the way back. I should have at least tried to get him to start talking. It would have been helpful to me as well. Everyone grieves differently. Maybe he needed the quiet. Maybe he was like me. Push it inside, into some secret place where all these memories dwell. Be sure and lock that door. Pray it never comes out.

I can't remember the last time I went swimming for fun. I can't relax around the pool if anyone is in the water. And I can't get that grandfather's face out of my head. Neither can I forget his beautiful granddaughter. Stories like this one are why you should never ask a first responder "What's the worst call you have ever made?"

Just so you know, this isn't it.

I met my little sister and her husband a few days ago. We were clearing out my brother's storage. After my mom died, we had put all his things in an 8x10 storage in the hope that one day he may want some of his stuff. His mental status has declined to the point where we decided that is never going to happen.

This small storage held all of his possessions with plenty of room left over. It was depressing to me to think that the things he held near and dear were about to be donated to Goodwill or thrown out in the trash.

High school yearbooks, his army uniform, and knickknacks he accumulated over the years filled totes and boxes.

The only furniture was a dresser and nightstand from his bedroom, and his headboard. There was a box of clothes that are much too big for him now. The last tote had sheets and towels from my mom's house. A lot of memories in a small space.

My sister, Barbara, was very diligent in going through any papers or documents we came across. His Birth Certificate was one of the only things she found that is important. The big surprise for me was several 35mm cameras. Apparently, Don liked to take pictures. One of the other surprises was a number of pictures of nieces and nephews. He never seemed to be sentimental about those type of things. Baby pictures and a timeline of these kids as they grew up, team pictures from sports, and events like graduations and weddings. I was shocked. Don and I shared a bedroom growing up and a last name, but I really didn't know him. Now he doesn't know me.

I find myself wondering if he ever had regrets about the life he missed out on. Never having a wife or kids of his own. Never owned a home or had any real friends. He had a mobile home for a short period of time but seemed to be happier living with my mom. I think the only time he stayed at the mobile home was when my oldest nephew stayed with him. I don't believe he was comfortable alone.

When he was stationed in Germany, he bought a cuckoo clock. It hung in my mom's living room for years. I'm not sure when they took it down but now it sits in a box in my garage. I will see if any of the kids want it. He had another surprise at the bottom of one of the totes. He had a picture of me in my Fire Department uniform in a frame. I don't have any pictures of any of my siblings unless they are on my phone.

I have one memory of Becky and I giving him a Christmas present. He loved to shop at Tractor Supply, so we gave him a gift card from there and a pocketknife. I just remember the look on his face. He was already living with my mom, and I don't believe that she even put up a tree. When I gave him his gift, he got emotional. Like I said before, we were never close. Maybe for a few minutes he felt like we were. I was such a sorry big brother. After I had moved out, I very seldom visited. My mom would make me angry, so I avoided even being around her. That also meant I rarely saw him. I've said before, I didn't "dislike" him. I just didn't really have any feelings for him. Good or bad. I feel guilty for that now.

The mental health issues he is dealing with seem to be accelerating rapidly. You can see the signs of cognitive decline on each visit. I'm uncomfortable seeing him this way, but I would feel even worse leaving Barbara alone to go see him. The visits are mentally draining, and physically exhausting. Barbara and Don are the closest in age, and probably the closest of the siblings. I think another thing that makes me feel guilty is that I'm older than he is, but I've been blessed with good health and a family of my own. I feel like he got cheated out of so many of the good things in life. He had no control over the hereditary portion of his condition, and he made some bad, or at least unhealthy choices of his own. I often wonder if he could do his life all over again, knowing how this is impacting his quality of life, would he make better choices, or was all his inevitable?

I'm so thankful for Barbara. She is an angel. An advocate for all his needs and care. She keeps in constant contact with the nurses and doctors in charge of his case.

She knows how he responds to certain meds, and she knows how to calm him and shows him love, even when he is angry or difficult to deal with. She has that gift. She does all these things while taking care of her own family and working in a busy career. I'm ashamed to say that he may be living on the street if I were the one responsible for his care. I try to always tell her how much I appreciate all she does for him. I thank God for her daily. I believe she will get her reward in Heaven for all her efforts. I love you, Barbara.

I pray for Don as well. I hope he is comfortable in his room. I'm not necessarily wishing that he would pass away, but I never want him to suffer. I think he has done enough of that. Even with his own issues to deal with, he took care of my mom. That could not have been easy. They were totally dependent on each other. For everything. In the last year of her life, she could not have taken care of herself. I believe the only thing that kept her going was the belief that he could not make it without her! She passed away shortly after Barbara had assured her that Don was getting the help he needed. Her job was done.

Don gets emotional when he asks to see his mom. He was at her funeral, and at that time he knew she had passed. He sat close to me at her service, but just seemed lost. Even though he sat that close, he asked Becky where I was. He had just started to slip mentally. Recently he asked Barbara if our mom was outside in the car. He has asked in the past why she doesn't visit him. Some people tell us it's best NOT to tell him she's gone. Some say to just gently remind him. Who knows which way is best. I really don't believe there is a "one size fits all' answer. I just wish he could feel peaceful with all of it.

Then There Were Three

The first three of us, Brenda, myself, and then Don, were far enough apart in age to ever foster really close ties. Don and Barbara were only 15 months apart and I believe that gave them a certain bond the rest of us missed out on. Growing up, I had a fairly close relationship with Brenda. She taught me how to drive, and I got to go places with her and her boyfriend David. She and David have been married for 51years. We used to talk a lot and I miss that. We went almost 30 years with no contact between us. Life has thrown us back together again. The last time I saw Brenda was almost 2 years ago at our mom's funeral. I spoke to her a few nights ago with an update on Don's condition. It was such a powerful conversation. It's almost like we had never been apart. The only big difference was our goodbye.

After almost 65 years on earth, I finally told Brenda that I love her. I just recently told Barbara that same thing.

So, can anybody tell me why those 3 little words can be so hard to say? I tell Becky I love her all the time. Rocky may not understand the words, but I know he feels loved. I tell my closest friends that I love them. And I really mean it. I have just recently reconnected with my cousin, and I always end with "I love you." But not with my own family? It doesn't make sense. Maybe you had a similar upbringing. Maybe the affection was non-existent for you as well. Hopefully not, but if it was, how has your life changed? Personally, I'm very affectionate with those closest to me. But sometimes not as much with those that should be in my familial circle. I told my dad on his deathbed. I don't think I ever told my mom. I know that I never told Don. I will never let another phone call or any conversation end without telling my sisters that I love them. Very much.

Most of this came up very recently. Don has been in a nursing home almost as long as my mom has been gone. Some of the things I've written about have been about Don and his struggles, or about my relationship with my mom. Just recently, Don aspirated in the nursing home. He was taken to the hospital and diagnosed with double pneumonia. Upon arrival at the hospital, he was weak, confused, and non-verbal. The attending physician asked if he had a DNR. Yes, he does. The doctor advised securing "comfort care" and possibly hospice. Barbara went to work taking care of these things for Don. The realization that the end may be near was quickly brought to our attention. Over the next several days I learned that my sisters and I had been praying the same prayer. "Please God, don't let Don suffer. Keep him free from pain. Please let him have the peace that only you can provide". He spiked a fever of 105 on his first day back. Hospice was brought in to begin caring for him. So, I thought I could prepare myself for the inevitable.

Barbara and her husband had visited Don when he first got out of the hospital. I went by the next day to express my concern about some highly insensitive comments made by an employee to my sister. After addressing that issue, I was asked if I wanted to see him. All my prior visits had been when Barbara was there. This would be the first time for me to see him alone.

I had seen Don for his birthday in May. The decline physically and mentally was sobering. I never had expectations of him getting better. I knew he would never recover his prior mental, or physical status. I guess in my mind, he would exist in a holding pattern. Barbara told me how bad he looked after the pneumonia, but I failed to really listen. Now, on my visit, there was no denying the truth. Standing there alone and looking at him, I finally accepted the fact that his fight was almost over.

I was at work when I got a text from Barbara that he had passed. It was around 3:30 in the afternoon on Thursday, July 27th. When I called Barbara back, she told me Brenda was with him when he took his last breath. Then it all made sense. All three of us had visited in his last days. Each in our own way had said goodbye. I believe he held on until he had seen all of us. I would give anything to see his reunion with my mom.

RIP Don. I will see you again.

There are two pictures that I've seen lately. One is of all of us kids. We are all smiling, we all look happy. The other one is visually more powerful. Don and I are sitting in a wagon. He looks to be about 2-3 years old. I'm sitting behind him with my arm wrapped around him, so he won't fall. Somewhere along the way I let him go.

We shared the middle bedroom in my childhood home. Early on it was bunkbeds and we couldn't see each other. Later we used them as twin beds and now we just ignored each other. We very seldom spoke. I don't really know why. I didn't dislike him. We never had big arguments or fights. We were just different. Radically.

I used to feel sorry for myself because I was only 16 when my dad died. It never dawned on me that Don was 13 and Barbara was only 12. Brenda was already married and had started a family. Three weeks

after my 18th birthday, I left to start my own. Once I left, I very seldom went back. Barbara had adjusted as well as could be expected. Don had adjusted, but not in a positive way.

Maybe it was during those years that Barbara and Don developed a bond. In these last several years, Barbara has become Don's legal guardian. In reality, she has been his guardian angel. She has carried the load in providing him care, putting his affairs in order, and with visiting him numerous times. She would speak kindly to him when he was agitated or confused. She could calm him with her words. I can't thank her enough for everything she has done.

Brenda provided love and financial support. I have to say, Don and I were both lucky to have two beautiful and loving sisters. God certainly knew what he was doing when he put us all together. Even though Don, and to some extent, my mom, would be unlikely choices to bring siblings closer together, that's exactly what they have done. My mom and Don lived together and relied on each other for everything. They have certainly brought my two sisters and I into a much more loving relationship. In these last few days, I have finally told both of them that I love them. I regret that I never told Don.

RIP Don. I will see you again. I love you.

Ever since I first started putting these thoughts on paper, I have wondered how to close it out. Not really the kind of writing that would warrant a cliffhanger. I can't just stop. What if I tell you this has been the most incredible experiment for me. It has brought me both comfort and pain. I have shared accomplishments and exposed my own flaws and shortcomings. If anything, I've written seems boastful, I apologize. That was never my intent. I was trying to share the joys I have had in this life. Mostly, when I read these pages, I feel blessed. And I find more reasons to be thankful. And humble. My cousin described me as "gentle". 15-20 years ago that would have upset me. I constantly worked to be strong. Physically, mentally, and emotionally strong. Now I understand that "gentle" is what was needed.

Anyone I ever responded to help needed gentle treatment. I've come to the realization that "gentle" is a different kind of strength. So my prayer for you I that God bless you with good health, love and kindness, and the strength to always be gentle. Amen

Till next time

One of the enormous benefits I received from my career as a firefighter has been meeting and working with such incredible people. I would like to introduce one of those people to you now.

Callie Crow came to teach a first aid course to the volunteer fire department in my part of the county. Most of the volunteers here are older and I was concerned about how they would relate to a female instructor. My fears were put to rest as Callie not only held their attention but demonstrated her skill as an instructor by having the entire class pass both the written and skills portions. Sometime later, I saw a post about Callie on social media. I'm going to let Callie tell her story as only she can.

I'm pledging my support to the non-profit she started. 10% of the profits from the book will go to help the cause. Incredible people doing lifesaving things.

Allow me to introduce you to my good friend, Callie Crow

Before I talk to you about his death, let me begin with his life. Allow me to introduce you to my son, Drew. Drew was 27 years old and a student at the University of North Texas studying political journalism. He was married, 6 foot 4 inches tall with huge cowboy boots, that he in fact adored. Drew loved steak and anything with substance. Drew was born an old man. My mom and I labeled him as that from the time he was able to communicate. He had this inert knowledge that was so obvious.

He was quirky, passionate, and told horrible corny jokes. Drew was sweet, kind, and lit up every room with his exaggerated smile. He had the most beautiful color of skin in which he referred to as "milk chocolate" at the ripe age of 4. But Drew also had a dependence on opioids. That addiction began 10 years earlier. You do the math. 27-10 =17. 17 is very young to be a drug addict, but the drug use actually began at the age of 14. I have never touched a drug in my entire life. I've never even smoked pot. I can tell you the times I've had alcohol in my body on one hand. In my mind, with this fact alone, my children were exempt from addiction. "That" only happens to parents who expose their children to such an environment. "That" only happens to people who don't love their children enough. It can't happen to me because I have spent my life and career serving the community. I was a great mother and apparently invincible. Except, I wasn't.

June 10th 2020, just before midnight I plopped on my bunk from exhaustion. I was at EMS station #2in Granbury Texas. I have been a paramedic for almost 20 years but have spent 25 years in the emergency medical services. I lived and breathed for my 3 children, Drew, MadiKate, and Gabe. It had already been a tough year. I had lost both of my young dogs, filed for divorce 2 months prior, and Covid was rocking everyone's world. My phone rang. I glanced down and it was a call from Drew. Before I even said hello, I heard Drew's wife screaming into the phone. I listened closer and heard the first responders in panic mode. I then began to hear the very distinct sound of the Lucus device. If you are unfamiliar with the Lucus, it's a device we carry in the ambulance to assist us during a cardiac arrest. A phenomenal invention that performs compressions and allows us, as first responders, to have our hands free to work on other ways to save the person's life. The patient's hands are attached by Velcro to the machine to allow for easy movement of the patient. I was certain I felt my soul leave my body in that very moment as I understood what this meant. I hung up the phone and left the station. I went directly home to get my daughter, Madi, who at the time was barely 23 years old. We drove an hour to the emergency room where they had taken my Drew. I stood in full uniform at the front desk, begging to go help save my baby. I was denied over and over. Remember, it was at the peak of Covid, and everything was changing in the hospital world. No families were allowed access, even in full uniform, and with a dying child on the other side of the door. Eventually I made it to the back. As I walked

through the resuscitation room door, my worst nightmare lay in front of me. Drew, unconscious, intubated, lines and tubes everywhere, and then there was the Lucus. Drew's arms hugged the device as his hands lay across the top of the machine, wrapped in place. The very last thing I remember that night was the blinding light reflected off his wedding band as I walked through the door. He lived for 36 more hours in the ICU. Again, because of Covid, I wasn't allowed much access to him, but the moments I did spend laid the groundwork of something very unexpected.

June 12th, 2020, just before 2:00 pm I sat on Drew's left side, grasping his cold, swollen, and pale hand. I loved his hands. There wasn't a lot of obvious DNA that had come from me in Drew, but his hands were identical to mine. Although a much larger version, we had the same lines and the same shape. I treasured this proof that he was mine. Slowly throughout the previous night and early morning, I began receiving information about the events of the night of Drew's overdose. Although I inserted my own assumptions on some of the details, I had a picture of the scene. Drew was at home with his wife, Adriana. He had just taken a shower and laid on their bed. Adriana had her back to him as she was working on the computer on some school assignments. They had been chit chatting and then he stopped responding.

She assumed he had dozed off until a few minutes later she noticed he was snoring and gurgling. She then saw he was pale and sweating. These are very classic signs of an opioid overdose. She shook him and shouted his name. Nothing. Frantically she dials 911 but could only scream in horror and shock. With this type of situation, it becomes labeled an" unknown problem" and the Calvary is sent out. The typical practice is a police officer or more will arrive first on scene to ensure it is safe for additional responding units such as EMS and/or the fire department. A city police officer arrived on scene within minutes of the call. The officer was carrying Narcan, a drug that has the potential to block the effects of an opioid and allow a person to regain consciousness and breathe on their own. Upon arrival, Drew was found still breathing slowly and with a pulse. With these conditions it is the optimal opportunity to utilize Narcan. For reasons I will never know, the officer did not deploy the Narcan. Because of scene safety issues, EMS and other first responders did not arrive before Drew went into cardiac arrest, which resulted in Drew's demise.

I knew we were down to the last moments. Adriana sat on Drew's right side playing his favorite playlist. I watched her closely, recognizing she was oblivious to all the signs of death. It's easy to forget that most people don't deal with death daily like I had for so many years. My mom sat in the corner of the room working on a crossword puzzle with the view of her first grandson dying on the bed purposely blocked. She dared not look in any direction other than the other way. I didn't blame her. I wanted to find a hole to die in. I watched the imagined scene play out in my mind like a never-ending movie reel. I could see the officer's thoughts each time the reel played. He would glance down at his Narcan pouch and then look at Drew laying there. The first time I saw it play, the officer's response was, "Oh, yeah, another druggy. I'll just wait for EMS." The next time he glanced at his Narcan pouch and then at Drew, he said, "oh yeah, I wonder if this is an overdose, but I never really got trained on this stuff and I can't remember how to do it." The next, "I don't want to give it to him, and it hurt him, so I'll just wait." I screamed "GIVE IT!!!" each time the reel played in my mind. I couldn't shut it off. I squeezed Drew's hand and began to cry. Both Adriana and my mom quickly noticed and were beginning to understand the progression. Adriana left the room and my mom continued to pretend there was something very interesting happening outside the window. I yelled at Drew in my mind. So angry at the way this was ending. The word "PURPOSE" rang through my head. I quickly denied the thought. It continued to infiltrate.

That's when the "conversation" began. There was a dialogue happening in my head that I now understand but wasn't actually conscious of at the time. "This is not the purpose I assigned to you Drew". I spoke to him then softly in my mind. We as parents somehow believe we are entitled to assign our children their purposes. That is laughable to me now. What do we say when our children are born or when we are watching them grow up? We say "When   grows up he/she will be a   and do this and that to save the world...blah, blah, blah..." We all do it. We think we deserve at least that. I mean, we are the ones that created them after all. HA! We plan out their lives and then the universe laughs at all of us! This went on for a bit until Drew spoke back. Yes, I said that he "spoke back" but not in the literal sense. I do not have the words or brain power to try to explain any of this really, but I will do my best. The words I was "hearing" were not words but feelings. Feelings coming directly from my son who lay dying in front of me. The world went black all around me and I had no choice but to listen. He told me that I was not allowed to choose his purpose, but I was allowed to do with it what I wanted to do with it. "It's yours now." "Go, you will see." I was certain I was losing my entire mind. I screamed "WAIT!" so loudly in my head that my mom, sitting in the corner, suddenly became restless. I stared at Drew's hand, denying the monitor's sudden alarms. In that very moment, he left. The peace that followed, I will never have the ability to explain. We all left within minutes, and it was over.

We were quickly asked to make decisions about the burial arrangements. Meanwhile my mind was downloading an entire blueprint. Suddenly, I was equipped with capabilities I had never possessed before. I didn't care to make the stupid burial arrangements! I had work to do! My brain began to flood with this new information. I sat in the ICU family consult room with my head in my hands. I'm sure it looked like I was grieving and certainly overwhelmed by Drew's death, but that wasn't what was happening at all. I was building what is now known as Drews27Chains. In that moment, it would have made sense to pick up my phone and call MadiKate and Gabe and let them know Drew did not make it. Instead, I began calling every single police officer I knew, "Do you carry Narcan? Were you trained? How long ago? Do you always carry? Do you know what an opioid overdose looks like? Who can you give it to? When do you administer? How do you administer?" And in those conversations, I received all the wrong answers. The first few days passed, and each breath was a painful reminder that my baby was gone. The funeral came and went. I was so blessed to have my mom, MadiKate, and Gabe right there with me. Mom moved most of her things to my house. We lived in our grief together, and mom and I haven't separated since. I woke up with apparent amnesia every morning for weeks. I would wake forgetting that Drew was dead. Open my eyes, look around, and then here it came! Like a jackhammer to the chest. Th tears shed during that time are unmeasurable. Have you ever been dehydrated from crying? I have, but I am here to tell you there is beauty in all things.

DREWS 27 CHAINS

November 24, 2020, Drews27Chains became an official non-profit organization. I began this organization with the blueprint given to me from Drew. I am a paramedic. I can jump in the back of an ambulance and help anyone, anytime! What I am NOT is a businessperson, a public speaker, or anyone that has experience with a non-profit organization. Except now, I'm all of these things. Drew gave me the most beautiful gift a mother could ever ask for; a child with an incredible purpose that will impact the entire world! Is it the same purpose that I had assigned him? No, far from it, but I wouldn't change a single thing.

Drews27Chains' mission and focus was to educate every first responder on recognition of opioid overdose, and the proper use of naloxone (Narcan). I began travelling locally to police departments and fire departments asking to do a 1-hour presentation and leave them with a supply of naloxone in hopes that no other family would have to experience the same loss we had just weeks before. The word quickly spread amongst local departments. I then began travelling all over the great state of Texas training on my days off. My mom generously donated money to the organization so I could continue my mission. Soon, I was so busy training and telling Drew's story, I needed to quit work and dedicate myself to the organization full time. This was challenging to say the least. No funding, no way to obtain free naloxone, but an undying passion that drove me every day. I spent every waking hour forming solid training, staying active on social media to tell Drew's story, networking with folks across the state, meeting with other families who had lost a loved one, and sending naloxone to anyone who asked for it. Then, the stories of people that had been saved with the naloxone given to them by someone who attended our training, started flowing into our inbox! Then there were stories of saves made by people who received naloxone from the Drews27Chains naloxone send out program. Look at you, Drew! Each day, each story, each training, each recovering addict or family member that called to thank me, put all the broken pieces back together.

In 2022, the organization started branching out beyond first responders and began training school districts, universities, churches, convenience stores, restaurants, partnering with community organizations, and travelling nationwide. The media was soon knocking on my door, and the requests for interviews were a constant flow. There were podcasts, radio programs, on camera interviews, newspaper articles, conference speaking events, and we were nominated and received multiple awards. I even began consulting for a pharmaceutical company that has a naloxone product. Drew's cowboy boots always in tow. MadiKate and Gabe were soon back on their feet and living their young lives. They missed their brother very much, but also gleamed with pride knowing they had a very special brother with a very important purpose. The saves and successes continued throughout 2023 as we educated and distributed lifesaving tools. In August, I was invited to the White House. I spent Overdose Awareness Day with the White House staff and specifically the ONDCP staff. Drew was honored at the event and his picture now hangs in the office of the ONDCP.

I have gained way more than I ever deserved through the life and death of my Drew.

January 8, 2024, Drews27Chains became worldwide as we travelled to Antigua to teach at the American Medical School of Antigua how to be prepared to save a life with recognition of an opioid overdose and the administration of naloxone. Setting foot outside the United States to talk about Drew is nothing short of a dream come true. I spent hours on the beach with Drew's boots absorbing the beauty of the land and truly appreciating the path that was given to us. The tears of grief have never stopped, but the pain is eased with the pride of knowing the waves Drew has created. I often wonder, "Can you see this, Drew? Do you see what you are doing??" He sends confirmation in many ways. Our bond has always been unbreakable, but now, it is much more than it has ever been. Life and death have a much different meaning to me now. I see everything with new eyes. I feel everything with a new heart. Drew has saved 63 lives as I write this. There are many we are unaware of, and many more to come! We all have a purpose. I understand this with great intensity now. You must be willing to see, not just look.

Callie Crow

(As this was being was being put in the book, I asked for the most recent number of saves. It is now 72!)

Gary Lee

"The two most important days in your life are the day you were born and the day you find out why."

Mark Twain

Acknowledgements

I feel certain I will leave someone, or several someone's, out of this portion of the book. Not on purpose, but because there have been so many that have helped along the way. Some have helped from day one, and many others came around when I stalled or stumbled. There has been one that has been here every day. Not just of this book, but of my life. None of this would ever have been possible without God. So first, and foremost, Thank you, God! Thank you for putting the words in my head, and for putting the feelings in my heart. Thank you for putting the people in my life that brought this story to life. Thank you for your impeccable timing, always putting the right person there, good or bad, to keep me focused. Thank you for your unconditional love, and for all the blessings you so freely give me. Not just during this time, but for all my life! All praise belongs to you, Father.

Now, for all my worldly helpers. Family and friends that have encouraged me, deciphered my scribbled notes, and helped me make sense of all of this. A special thank you to the ones that have patiently dealt with my caveman efforts on the computer! From day one, many years ago, I have handwritten all my notes. Printed. Even I couldn't read my own cursive! The words sometimes pour into my head faster than I could put them on paper. Words were scratched through, corrections in the margins, or sometimes just left out. It's definitely been a work of love. I greatly appreciate all the people that have helped me. Let me tell you about them.

To my beautiful wife, Becky. Thank you for believing in me enough to let me follow this dream, and for suffering through my impatience with all things technical! I love you, Baby girl! For my beautiful cousin, Mary Birdwell, for kick starting this whole experience. Mary is a published author, and it was her encouragement that convinced me to make this attempt. Thank you, Mary, for answering all my questions, and for allowing me to vent when things weren't flowing the way I wanted, and especially for loving me! I love you right back!

I couldn't or wouldn't have reached this point without the help of one of my dearest friends, Tana Thomas. When Tana and her husband Steve first moved here, she and Becky quickly became friends. Steve and Tana are the epitome of true friends. Both possess a "servant's heart", a warm and compassionate spirit, and are the least judgmental people I've ever met. Steve graciously allowed me to impose on their time when I asked Tana if she would help me with typing and proofreading. She did so much more than that. Tana read things that I've never shared with anyone. She saw raw, emotional things, but never thought less of me for showing that side of myself. Steve is the most positive Christian influence in my life. More than any preacher, Sunday school teacher, or any of my family or friends. He has a quiet, caring heart. He has never "preached" to me. His influence is by example. Without saying a word, he inspired me to read the Bible, cover to cover, and really listen to what it has to say. Saying Thank you to this incredible couple will never be enough. I love you both!

As the words in the body of the book began pouring out, my cousin Mary advised me to find someone to write a Foreword for the book. As soon as she said it, I knew who I wanted to ask. A dear friend of mine, Landon Stallings, is truly one of a kind. We are both retired from the Fort Worth Fire Department and his son attended high school in the small town we live in. Landon is exceptionally bright and could have been successful in any field. Instead of pursuing any other occupation and the higher pay they would bring, he chose a profession of service.

Another of my friends with a "servant's heart!" I had to have complete trust in someone to be able to share my idea of this book. I was nervous to ask because I know he stays busy. He put me at ease and almost made me feel like I was doing him a favor! You see what I mean about God putting people in my life at the right time and right place? Thank you, Landon, for not only writing the Foreword, but for expressing it all so well! Maybe the next book should be yours! A special thanks for so many years of being a great friend.

I'm sure there are people that have written books by themselves. I'm also sure that I never could. There is so much more to do than just putting everything on paper. As I neared completion, once again, my cousin Mary, pointed me in the right direction and helped me find a publishing company. For some reason, I put off making that call. It's one thing to have your family or friends see what you have been writing. It's a whole other animal to share it with a stranger. That's even compounded by the fact that the people now looking at your writing have tons of things come across their desks. All types of writing. Putting my words in front of strangers makes me feel completely vulnerable, exposed to any ridicule, hoping and praying for accreditation. I have been fortunate to be associated with Palmetto Publishing. My first contact was with Reese Walker. Once again, God put me in touch with just the one I needed. As I dialed, the sweaty palm feeling of public speaking was all I felt. I could not have picked a better first contact! Reese put me at ease and answered all my questions without making me feel inept. I truly appreciate all her help and was sad to move on to a project manager. That sadness was short lived. I was then contacted by Elizabeth Stallman. She has been another Godsend! Elizabeth has been incredibly patient with me and has been a great source of both information and encouragement. I hope Reese and "Liz", know how much I appreciate all they have done for me. Thank you both!

Every time I thought I was nearly finished, a little voice in my head would whisper, "Not yet." I'm not normally a patient person, so sometimes it was frustrating, to say the least. Maybe it's the title of my next book!! Mary rescued me once again. She advised me to find someone to help me with a book cover. Becky helped me start looking for someone artistic, but none of those felt right. Becky's co-worker, Stephanie Rouse recommended a local artist, Laura Butler. When I contacted her by phone, I knew she was the one. When I met her in person, I was sure I had made the right choice. I told Laura that I wish she could look in my ear and see the picture in my head. Sitting with her was like visiting a dear friend. She listened to my attempt to describe the picture I wanted. The first image she sent me to consider gave me goosebumps! She has a gift, not just an artistic one. She is a wonderful listener, and an incredible soul. Thank you, Laura, for being so willing to help me. And thank you Stephanie, for the reference.

I'm sure there are others I forgot to thank. Many of my friends and neighbors have heard that I was attempting to write this book. I have had more encouragement and good luck wishes from them than I can count. To anyone I may have forgotten to mention: I promise I remember everything you have done for me. All the kind words, all the support, all the love. I also promise that at the time you did anything for me, I thanked God for putting you in my life. May God bless you all! Thank you!

About the Author

Gary Lee, the author of *Son of a Carpenter*, is a retired Battalion Chief from the Fort Worth Fire Department. Now residing west of Fort Worth, he enjoys a peaceful retirement with his loving wife, Becky, and their rescue dog, Rocky. Embracing his new chapter, Gary spends his days appreciating the beauty of nature and the company of his friends and neighbors. His life, filled with blessings, inspires his writing. His experiences as a firefighter and his current lifestyle in a small town resonate in his work, making it relatable for fellow first responders and those interested in their unique lifestyle.